*The Best Kept Secrets of Intercession
& Other Types of Prayer*

MARNITHA ANN HORN

Copyright © 2019 by Marnitha Horn.
All rights reserved. No part of this book may be reproduced, scanned, or distributed in any printed or electronic form without permission.

All scripture references are taken from the Amplified Version of the Bible unless otherwise noted.

First Edition: March 2019
Printed in the United States of America

Dedication

This book is dedicated to Daddy God. Without your guidance and love for me, this book would not be possible. Thank you for your constant encouragement and never ceasing love. I am who I am because of You.

Acknowledgments

To Evangelist Dorothy Lee McCullough, Mama you are no longer here, but rest assured you are among the great cloud of witnesses. I salute you Mama. Your prayers are still active in the earth realm. I love you girl, until we meet again on the other side.

To my one and only daughter, LeroSandra TaNeal McCullough "aka" Shauny. Your Love for me has never been doubted. You are a "REAL BOSS" AND A REAL DRILL SERGEANT! I think you and Coach Sophia are family because you both like to push people into their destinies. Thank you for the constant encouragement I LOVE YOU TO LIFE!

To Coach Sophia Ruffin, it's you that planted a seed in me that I could write books and look at me now, I'm doing what you saw. THANKS COACH SOPHIA, THE "REAL COMEBACK KID" and a real "BOSS IN THE SPIRIT REALM".

To Mother Christine McGlothin Moore, your love for me is unmatched. Thanks for being in my life and loving me right where I was. You saw this day before I did, actually you prophesied to me on my last visit in Cincinnati and it has come to fruition. Thank you for pushing me.

To my friend Pastor Kimberly Gragston. It was you that gave me my first platform in 2010 in Hilton Head, South Carolina. I had never taught on such a large platform, but thank you for trusting the God in me and allowing me to stand before the masses and to teach the word of God.

To my spiritual sisters- Myra Clarke, Sandra Cook, Perda Harris, Delores Oliver and Jeanette King. We have labored during the fourth watch of prayer day after day, week after week, month after month and year after year. You have pushed me to go deeper in prayer and I thank you. Your faithfulness to God and intercession is unmatched. We've prayed while sick, on vacations, in airports and on the way to work. I can never THANK YOU ENOUGH.

To a man that needs no introduction, Dr. Anthony Earl. One of your favorite sayings is that the mind mimics what it sees. Well I believe you are correct. I learned my studying of scripture from you as I formatted this book. I realize that it's a teaching manual on prayer. You could always be found sitting with multiple books at one time on the table in the kitchen at City Church International. Thank you for every prayer and word of encouragement. All I can say is, "Look at me now."

To Apostle C.J. and Prophetess Kim Stokes, my brother and sister in the Gospel, thanks for giving me the opportunity to stand before your sheep in your house on your platform, and to pour out what God poured into me. I shall never forget your love and your sacrifices for me.
To Pastor Mattie Matthews, your trust in the God in me has never gone unnoticed, Thanks Mama Pastor for your unconditional love and sacrifice. You've also given me a platform where I could stand and say what God had given to me for the people. I salute you woman of righteousness and holiness.

To my Ordained of God church family, you guys have loved me unconditionally since day one. Thank you for making me feel right at home.

To Apostle Kenneth Rhymes "aka" Dad and Prophetess Jacqueline Rhymes "aka"Mama, thank you for every prophetic release over my life and ministry; and thank you for having my back in ministry. You have never allowed me to go out to do ministry without first praying and laying hands on me. Thank you for your apostolic grace and covering over me as I launch out even further in the things of the Kingdom.

Table of Contents

Foreword	i
Introduction	1
The Book of Genesis	6
The Book of Exodus	30
The Book of Numbers	46
The Book of Deuteronomy	54
The Book of Joshua	59
The Book of Judges	63
The Book of Ruth	80
The Book of 1 Samuel	82
The Book of 2 Samuel	94
The Book of 1 Kings	107
The Book 2 Kings	121
The Book of 1 Chronicles	129
The Book of 2 Chronicles	136
The Book of Ezra	151
The Book of Nehemiah	154
The Book of Esther	165
The Book of Job	167
The Book of Psalms	173
Types of Prayer Defined	176

Foreword

This book is a comprehensive and relatable study of scripture as it relates to prayer and intercession. It reflects the heart of an intercessor. Marnitha is a woman of prayer, and this is evident in her ability to research scriptures and unearth the pearls of prayer and intercession in the chapters she exegesis. Chapter after chapter she expounds in a way that both scholars and laymen can comprehend.

Marnitha is graced with the pen of the scribe. She writes with passion and love about the greatest intercessor ever known. She finds Him in Genesis and throughout each chapter. He is presented to us as Daddy God, a loving father, friend and confidant. The warmth you feel from reading this book will inspire you to run to Him. The personal touch that is given to Him in this book displays the great love He has for us regardless of our status.

Marnitha takes us on a journey through scripture meticulously dissecting each chapter where we find prayer interjected. As a good friend always says, "She gives us scholar for our holler." The depth of this read will compel you to study in a deeper place.

Through scripture, Marnitha unfolds the various ways God communicates with us. She takes to task the belief that prayer is not a ritual of special words and duty, but it is relational, progressive, and conversational.

Each chapter brings a curiosity that leads us to a new level of understanding that prayer is intertwined with everything God says and demonstrates in His Word. It leaves us with a hunger to know Him and love Him in a greater place of communication through prayer.

Marnitha skillfully gives definition for the various levels and dimension of prayer. You will be enriched and motivated as you read this powerful book. It will challenge you to study and upgrade your knowledge of God and connection with Him through prayer.

Apostle Kenneth and Prophetess Jacqueline Rhymes
Senior Pastors, Ordained of God Full Gospel Church

Foreword

It is with the greatest gratification that I propose the writings of this woman of God, Prophetess Marnitha Horn. God in His infinite wisdom and far-sightedness drops those with the heart of eternity into time who have heard the whispers of God in prayer. This book of prayer is stimulating, encouraging, and empowering to all who desire the will of God be fulfilled and to be catapulted into the predestined will God ordained just for them.

Marnitha is a seasoned woman of God, a prayer warrior, and a danger to hell every day her feet hit the floor. Marnitha is a traveling evangelist. I have been inspired by the anointing that flows from her when she preaches the Word of God.

Now under the auspices of the Holy Spirit, she is using yet another gift from God, the written word. These writings will give insight on scriptures admonishing the power of prayer. The readers of this book will never be the same.

Pastor Mattie Matthews
Executive Director
Daughters of Zelophehad & The Sons of Issachar

Foreword

I have pastored for over 25 years and have been blessed to serve many gifted people. I have learned that each one brought unique and precious gifts to help in my development. Life has taught me to look at things differently, especially those problematic and complex encounters.

Then there are those unique treasures that stand out the most. They are those individuals who are radiant and overflowing with personality and grace. Their infectious spirit lifts and inspires me to go the distance. Collectively all encounters can bring a wealth of insights that provide overcoming wisdom that paves the way to victory. We must pay close attention to the details of each relationship and extract their beautiful treasures.

Prayer has served me powerfully for 40 years in my walk with God. It has been a precious tool in helping me to overcome many obstacles and pitfalls in life. It has also helped me to chart my course and encounter some of the most fantastic experiences.

I have known Prophetess Marnitha Horn for over 20 years and have had the pleasure of serving as both her pastor and mentor for many of those years. She is one of those individual gems I spoke of earlier. She is an extraordinary person of prayer. Her fiery passion and commitment to intercede for others is breathtaking.

Her compilation of insights will provide the reader with the wisdom she has accumulated from over 30 years of walking with God. The most neglected weapon given to us is prayer. In her book, Marnitha shows us the intricacies of fervent effectual prayers.

We often find ourselves wrestling with many hard things in life. This book will empower you to understand your journey in Christ better and conquer those things that are designed to disrupt it. Marnitha serves as one of my most loyal and trusted prayer coverings. I believe that you too will find her work just as beneficial.

Dr. Anthony Earl, MDiv, DMin

Introduction

Let me begin by letting you in on a well-guarded secret. You may be asking yourself, what is it? Well I'm here to tell you something that everyone should know, but many don't, and that is that God is love. Yes, there it is, the secret is out. Daddy God is love and He loves us dearly. I wanted the foundation of this introduction to be about Daddy God's love. I think a lot of people don't talk to God because they feel He is unreachable and untouchable. They feel He is too busy running the universe, so surely He doesn't have time for them or that He just doesn't understand what they are going through. Wrong, wrong, and wrong again.

"For God so [greatly] loved and dearly prized the world, that He [even] gave His [One and] only begotten Son, so that whoever believes and trusts in Him [as Savior] shall not perish, but have eternal life." – John 3:16 AMP

Prayer is the number one way we communicate with Daddy God. It isn't a one-sided conversation. It is a two-way activity between you and God the Father. Our communication skills or lack there of do not bother Him. You may have a speech impediment, it's okay, it doesn't bother him in the least. You may say to yourself, "I don't have anything to say." Honey let me tell you, yes you do! If you have family members in prison, children acting out, you're not where you want to be in life or ministry, you have the desire to marry, your job isn't the best, or maybe you love everything about your life and everything is perfect, there is still much to talk to Daddy God about.

Daddy God has always been a conversationalist. He loves to talk. He loves to share. Daddy God is the parent you can come to when no one else will listen. He doesn't have to sleep nor does He need a power nap. Daddy God is always ready to hear from you. He is not the friend that you call because you need to talk but can never catch up with. Daddy God doesn't block your number when you call. Let me ease your mind by saying this, Daddy God is never so busy that He doesn't want to hear from you, so just reach out and talk to Him.

"He will not allow your foot to slip; He who keeps you will not slumber. Behold, He who keeps Israel will neither slumber [briefly] nor sleep [soundly]." - Psalm 121:3-4 AMP

You may find yourself having a bad day, week or month, it's okay, Daddy God understands. Never think you can't tell Daddy God something because He is going to be angry, that you'll be punished because you failed the same test again; or that you can't tell Daddy God that your old mindset may be returning. You can tell Daddy God that you're dealing with trust issues because you've been let down before, so it's really hard for you to trust anyone. You can tell him anything and everything.

"O Lord, you have searched me [thoroughly] and have known me. You know when I sit down and when I rise up [my entire life, everything I do]; You understand my thought from afar. You scrutinize my path and my lying down, And You are intimately acquainted with all my ways. Even before there is a word on my tongue [still unspoken],Behold, O Lord, You know it all. You have enclosed me behind and before, And [You have] placed Your hand upon me." – Psalm 139:1-5 AMP

Daddy God knows you better than you know yourself. He knows every aspect of your character. He knows the good, the bad, and the ugly. He's Daddy God so it's in His nature to know all things concerning His children. He's very understanding and very knowledgeable of who and what you are. Daddy God knows your potential, even when you don't think you have any. You may glance around at others in ministry and do a comparison study on you versus them, and you may say to yourself, "They've been in church a long time," or "Daddy likes them more than he likes me." Nope, none of this is true.

" Opening his mouth, Peter said: " Most certainly I understand now that God is not one to show partiality [to people as though Gentiles were excluded from God's blessing], but in every nation the person who fears God and does what is right [by seeking Him] is acceptable and welcomed by Him."
– Acts 10:34-35 AMP

You have a right to seek Him; and you have a right to go to Him as much as you like and as often as you need to. He's readily available. Nothing is too great or too small. Daddy God is love and He loves all of His children dearly. He wants you to bring everything you've been carrying to Him.

"Casting all your cares [all your anxieties, all your worries, and all your concerns, once and for all] on Him, for He cares about you [with deepest affection, and watches over you very carefully]." – 1 Peter 5:7 AMP

It doesn't matter what you may be facing or what may be trying to overtake you. Daddy God's line is never so busy that you can't reach out to Him. You can speak to Daddy God in your car, in the shower, at your job, and even in the grocery store. You never have to worry about seeing a sign that says, " Do not disturb." You have unlimited access to Daddy God's presence.

"For we do not have a High Priest who is unable to sympathize and understand our weaknesses and temptations, but One who has been tempted [knowing exactly how it feels to be human] in every respect as we are, yet without [committing any] sin. Therefore let us [with privilege] approach the throne of grace [that is, the throne of God's gracious favor] with confidence and without fear, so that we may receive mercy [for our failures] and find [His amazing] grace to help in time of need [an appropriate blessing, coming just at the right moment]."
– Hebrews 4:15-16 AMP

As you take this journey with me, I will introduce different types of prayers that you should be using on a consistent basis. No, all prayers are not the same. Though the overarching purpose for all prayer is to share your heart in conversation with Daddy God, and after you have shared, to listen intently for His response, there are strategic prayers that you should be praying for different situations. These types of prayers include: prayers of supplication, prayers of intercession, prayers of faith, prayers of agreement (corporate prayer), prayers of praise and thanksgiving, prayers of blessing, prayers of worship, prayers of lament, prayers in the Spirit, travailing prayers, and prophetic intercession.

Along with sharing different types of prayer, I will also share scriptures about men and women who were just like you and I. They were people who lied, cheated, stole, worshipped other gods, walked in unbelief, committed murder and even doubted God. We will revisit their lives, including the tests and trials they faced and the prayers that got them through and pulled them out of dark places. These prayers include those that moved God's hand to rescue many from a fate worse than death; and those that literally saved nations from annihilation. Prayers like those from Ishmael who was not the son of the promise, and who was cast out along with his mother; and prayers that opened the eyes of Elisha's servant so that he could see that there were more with them than with the enemy. Prayers that Elijah prayed when he asked that it not rain for three years; and prayers from Hannah, a woman barren, that she might conceive. Prayers that Esther prayed for her nation; prayers that David prayed after the loss of his son; and prayers that Hezekiah and Isaiah prayed concerning the threats of Sennacherib, the King of Assyria.

In looking at each of these men and women we will discover the necessity of prayer in the life of every believer. From their stories, my hope is that your faith will be built up and you will endeavor to become a more effective prayer warrior and intercessor. Okay, let's get going. It's time to fine-tune your prayer life.

Chapter One

The Book of Genesis

The Beginning of Prayer

"Eve conceived again and she bore Adam another son who they named Seth. Eve said God has given me another son to replace Abel who Cain had killed. Seth also bore a son who was named Enosh. At the time of Enosh's birth, men began to call on the name of the Lord and they worshipped the Lord and offered up praise and thanksgiving." – Genesis 4:25-26

After the loss of Abel at the hands of his brother Cain, God in his infinite wisdom gives Adam and Eve another son, whom they name Seth, which means anointed, compensation. God uses Seth to usher in a new dispensation of prayer through the birth of a son named Enosh. Upon his birth, men began to call on the name of the Lord and they worshipped the Lord who was the creator of all things. This had not been done since the fall of Adam. Men once again found their voices and used them to give God the glory.

Because we live in a fallen world, it's important that we keep our focus on the only one who can save us and sustain us. Prayer allows us to do just that-to take the focus off of ourselves and the calamity around us, and instead to put it where it matters most-on God. Prayer is an act of faith as it ultimately signifies our belief in God, and confirms our trust in His ability to both hear and answer us.

The Progression of Prayer

We meet Abram in the twelfth chapter of Genesis where God is conversing with him; and during this time with God, Abram is given directives that he is to follow.

"Now the LORD had said to Abram: "Get out of your country, From your family And from your father's house, To a land that I will show you. I will make you a great nation; I will bless you And make your name great; And you shall be a blessing. I will bless those who bless you, And I will curse him who curses you; And in you all the families of the earth shall be blessed." So Abram departed as the LORD had spoken to him, and Lot went with him. And Abram was seventy-five years old when he departed from Haran. Then Abram took Sarai his wife and Lot his brother's son, and all their possessions that they had gathered, and the people whom they had acquired in Haran, and they departed to go to the land of Canaan. So they came to the land of Canaan. Abram passed through the land to the place of Shechem, as far as the terebinth tree of Moreh. And the Canaanites were then in the land." -Genesis 12:1-6 NKJV

Abram's time with God is both a time of supplication and a time to receive instructions for the next stage of his life. The time he spends in prayer with God gives him the much needed faith and strength to follow through with the plans of God for his life and the lives of those that were with him. Being directed by a God that he could not see with the natural eye, but that he knew by faith existed, Abram was told to leave Haran and all that was familiar, and to go to a land that God would show him.

To supplicate means to petition or entreat someone for something. The prayer of supplication is the type of prayer that should be prayed by every believer. Often fueled by passionate zeal and hunger, the prayer of supplication is a push on the part of the believer to inquire of the Lord concerning every facet of their life. As we look at the prayer life of Abram, we see a desire on his part to know God more intimately. His prayers are driven by purpose. Just like Abram, we too must learn to trust God as we seek Him diligently.

Matthew 6:33 tells us, *"Seek first the kingdom of God and His righteousness, and all of these things shall be added to you."*

If we seek after God first and foremost, then He is faithful to answer. After receiving a message to leave everything that was familiar to him, Abram did just that. He didn't waver. He just did it. God may be asking you to take a leap of faith and walk away from the familiar to the unfamiliar. When you pray, follow His leading, and know above all else that He is up to something and He has you on His mind.

The Continuation of Prayer

"So Abram went up out of Egypt, he and his wife and all that he had, and Lot with him, into the South [country of Judah, the Negeb]. Now Abram was extremely rich in livestock and in silver and in gold. And he journeyed on from the South [country of Judah, the Negeb] as far as Bethel, to the place where his tent had been at the beginning, between Bethel and Ai, Where he had built an altar at first; and there Abram called on the name of the Lord. [Gal. 3:6-9.]" -Genesis 13:1-4 AMPC

Genesis 12:10 tells us that there was a famine in Canaan and that this famine was very grievous, but it doesn't say that Abram consulted God, it just says that he took all that he had and left Canaan temporarily for Egypt.

Because Abram didn't consult God on what should be done in the midst of the famine in Canaan, he goes to Egypt and this move sets in motion a chain of events that begins with lies. Abram and Sarai lie about the nature of their relationship, and in doing so they cause God's hand to move against Pharaoh and his household through very serious plagues. Pharaoh asks Abram why he lied and said that Sarai was his sister, when she was really his wife. He then tells Abram to take his wife and get out of his country; and gives a command to his men to make sure that they were escorted out of the land. Having been ordered to leave Egypt, Abram takes Sarai and all that they have and they go up from Egypt and make their way back into the south. Lot comes with them. Abram, during this period, had acquired great wealth, which included livestock, silver and gold. Continuing to where his tent had been prior, between Bethel and Ai, Abram calls on the name of the Lord.

Abram got caught in a lie, after making a move that had not been directed by God. One false move led to a series of bad decisions that yielded harsh consequences for many people. Yet, even in this, despite not getting it right this particular time, Abram does eventually seek God again.

Just like Abram, despite our mistakes or mishaps, we must continue to seek God. Don't allow one mistake to deter you from seeking after Him. Your prayer life is crucial not only to you, but to others as well.

Prayer Is Made In Regards to An Heir

Abram communed often with the Lord as he journeyed toward the south. Altars were built along the way to continue with his worship of God. By the time Abram got to Canaan, wherever he had a tent, God had an altar that was sanctified by prayer. He instructed those that were in his household to praise and worship the one true God, and insisted that seeking and calling upon God was to be a major part of their culture. Moving forward to the 15th chapter of Genesis we see the word of the Lord coming to Abram in a vision:

"After these things the word of the LORD came to Abram in a vision saying, "Do not be afraid, Abram. I am your shield, your exceedingly great reward." But Abram said, "Lord GOD, what will You give me, seeing I go childless, and the heir of my house is Eliezer of Damascus?" Then Abram said, "Look, You have given me no offspring; indeed one born in my house is my heir!" And behold, the word of the LORD came to him, saying, "This one shall not be your heir, but one who will come from your own body shall be your heir." Then He brought him outside and said, "Look now toward heaven, and count the stars if you are able to number them." And He said to him, "So shall your descendants be." And he believed in the LORD, and He accounted it to him for righteousness. Then He said to him, "I am the LORD, who brought you out of Ur of the Chaldeans, to give you this land to inherit it."" Genesis 15:1-7 NKJV

As we see in this passage, Abram was very concerned about himself and Sarai who were childless. According to the customs at that time, if Abram were to die and had no son, the eldest servant would become the rightful heir. This matter weighed very heavy upon Abram's heart, so we see him in prayer petitioning God concerning the matter. Take a really close look at God's response. God's response is that this one shall not be your heir. As I shared with you earlier, prayer is a two- sided conversation. When you are actively seeking God's counsel concerning a matter, PLEASE learn how to wait. He will answer in His timing. As the prayer shifts from Abram's petitions to God, we now hear the Father's response to the prayers that have been prayed. God takes over the conversation and informs Abram that his heir would come from his own body. God brings Abram outside and tells him to look up into the sky and number the stars, for that's how he was going to bless his descendants, so much so that Abram wouldn't be able to number them. Verse 6 says that Abram believed in the Lord and that God accounted it to him as righteousness.

When the opportunity presents itself and God speaks, let us take Abram's response to what he heard and apply it to our situation. Let's believe the Lord, so that it can be accounted to us as righteousness.

"Now Sarai, Abram's wife, had borne him no children. And she had an Egyptian maidservant whose name was Hagar. So Sarai said to Abram, "See now, the LORD has restrained me from bearing children. Please, go in to my maid; perhaps I shall obtain children by her." And Abram heeded the voice of Sarai. Then Sarai, Abram's wife, took Hagar her maid, the Egyptian, and gave her to her husband Abram to be his wife, after Abram had dwelt ten years in the land of Canaan. So he went in to Hagar, and she conceived. And when she saw that she had conceived, her mistress became despised in her eyes. Then Sarai said to Abram, "My wrong be upon you! I gave my maid into your embrace; and when she saw that she had conceived, I became despised in her eyes. The LORD judge between you and me." So Abram said to Sarai, "Indeed your maid is in your hand; do to her as you please." And when Sarai dealt harshly with her, she fled from her presence. Now the Angel of the LORD found her by a spring of water in the wilderness, by the spring on the way to Shur. And He said, "Hagar, Sarai's maid, where have you come from, and where are you going?" She said, "I am fleeing from the presence of my mistress Sarai." - Genesis 16:1-8 NKJV

I know that 10 years is 10 years, there's no other way to say it, but hear me good, GOD DOES NOT NEED OUR HELP! Sarai and Abram both had faith issues. Time was moving along and neither one of them were getting any younger, so they decided why don't we just help God out a little bit. In helping God out, Abram heeded the voice of Sarai.

According to the custom of the day, if a woman was barren and could not conceive, it was an acceptable practice to give your maidservant to your husband so that she could bear seed for you. Sarai does this and Hagar conceives a child by Abram, but she despises her mistress Sarai because she's with child and Sarai is still barren. Now Abram has to deal with two women that are at odds with one another. There is envy, jealousy and strife in the household. Sarai says to Abram, " My wrong be upon you!" In other words she's saying everything that has happened is Abram's fault. Sarai won't admit her wrong, so she blames Abram. What we see transpiring here in the sixteenth chapter of Genesis, we've seen before in the third chapter in the garden with Adam, Eve and the serpent.

In Genesis 3:9-14 NKJV God asks, "Adam where are you? Adam responds, "I heard your voice but I was afraid because I'm naked" God responds, "Who told you that you were naked? Have you eaten from the tree that I commanded you not to eat from?" Adam's response, "The woman whom you gave to be with me, she gave me of the tree and I ate. So God asks the woman, "What is this that you have done? Her response, "The serpent deceived me and I ate."

It's the blame game all over again. Nobody wants to own up to their wrongdoing. I have no doubt that Abram's altar, where He communed with God, was still there for use, but we don't read that he prayed to God.

What we do see is that when Sarai makes the request of him, he doesn't say, " Wait, let me go and inquire of the Lord and see what he has to say concerning the matter." Instead he heeds the wrong advice of Sarai which starts a chain reaction of bad events. Sarai becomes angry because Hagar conceives, so she mistreats her, which leads to Hagar running away. Hagar is then found by the angel of the Lord who tells her that she is with child and that his name would be Ishmael.

"The Angel of the LORD continued, "Behold, you are with child, And you will bear a son; And you shall name him Ishmael (God hears), Because the LORD has heard and paid attention to your persecution (suffering)." - Genesis 16:11 AMP

Hagar was a member of Abram's household. Their household may not have been perfect, but she knew enough of the one true God that she could call him and that he would indeed answer her prayers, so it is fitting that her son would be named GOD HEARS.

A Covenant Is Made Between Abram and God

"When Abram was ninety-nine years old, the LORD appeared to him and said, "I am God Almighty; Walk [habitually] before Me [with integrity, knowing that you are always in My presence], and be blameless and complete [in obedience to Me]. "I will establish My covenant (everlasting promise) between Me and you, And I will multiply you exceedingly [through your descendants]." Then Abram fell on his face [in worship], and God spoke with him, saying, "As for Me, behold, My covenant is with you, And [as a result] you shall be the father of many nations. "No longer shall your name be Abram (exalted father), But your name shall be Abraham (father of a multitude); For I will make you the father of many nations. I

will make you exceedingly fruitful, and I will make nations of you, and kings will come from you. I will establish My covenant between Me and you and your descendants after you throughout their generations for an everlasting covenant, to be God to you and to your descendants after you. I will give to you and to your descendants after you the land in which you are a stranger [moving from place to place], all the land of Canaan, as an everlasting possession [of property]; and I will be their God."" - Genesis 17:1-8 AMP

Fourteen years have passed since Genesis 16 and God appears to Abram and says," I am God Almighty, walk before me with integrity knowing that you are always in my presence and be blameless and in complete obedience to me. Then Abram falls on his face and worships."

Once circumstances had been fixed in the household, things were as they should be, altars were being used as intended, prayers were being offered up to God regularly, and petitions were made as well as Intercession for those that lived among them, God makes a covenant with Abram and promises to multiply him exceedingly through his descendants and that he would be a father of many nations. Abram receives a name change from Abram to Abraham, which means father of a multitude.

"Further, God said to Abraham, "As for you [your part of the agreement], you shall keep and faithfully obey [the terms of] My covenant, you and your descendants after you throughout their generations. This is [the sign of] My covenant, which you shall keep and faithfully obey, between Me and you and your descendants after you: Every male among you shall be circumcised. And you shall be circumcised in the flesh of your foreskins, and it shall be the sign (symbol, memorial) of the covenant between Me and you. Every male among you who is

eight days old shall be circumcised throughout your generations, [including] a servant whether born in the house or one who is purchased with [your] money from any foreigner, who is not of your descendants. A servant who is born in your house or one who is purchased with your money must be circumcised; and [the sign of] My covenant shall be in your flesh for an everlasting covenant. And the male who is not circumcised in the flesh of his foreskin, that person shall be cut off from his people; he has broken My covenant.""

- Genesis 17:9-14 AMP

A covenant between God and Abraham is made in Genesis 17:9-14. This is a binding contract cut in blood. Abraham was to circumcise every male who was eight days old, including servants, whether born in the house or purchased with money. God's part was to give him descendants like the stars in the heavens, make nations of him and to bring forth kings from him.

"Then God said to Abraham, "As for Sarai your wife, you shall not call her name Sarai (my princess), but her name will be Sarah (Princess). I will bless her, and indeed I will also give you a son by her. Yes, I will bless her, and she shall be a mother of nations; kings of peoples will come from her." Then Abraham fell on his face and laughed, and said in his heart, "Shall a child be born to a man who is a hundred years old? And shall Sarah, who is ninety years old, bear a child?" And Abraham said to God, "Oh, that Ishmael [my firstborn] might live before You!" But God said, "No, Sarah your wife shall bear you a son indeed, and you shall name him Isaac (laughter); and I will establish My covenant with him for an everlasting covenant and with his descendants after him. As for Ishmael, I have heard and listened to you; behold, I will bless him, and will make him fruitful and will greatly multiply him [through his descendants]. He will be the father of twelve princes

(chieftains, sheiks), and I will make him a great nation. But My covenant [My promise, My solemn pledge], I will establish with Isaac, whom Sarah will bear to you at this time next year." And God finished speaking with him and went up from Abraham. Then Abraham took Ishmael his son, and all the servants who were born in his house and all who were purchased with his money, every male among the men of Abraham's household, and circumcised the flesh of their foreskin the very same day, as God had said to him. So Abraham was ninety-nine years old when he was circumcised. And Ishmael his son was thirteen years old when he was circumcised. On the very same day Abraham was circumcised, as well as Ishmael his son. All the men [servants] of his household, both those born in the house and those purchased with money from a foreigner, were circumcised along with him [as the sign of God's covenant with Abraham]."
- Genesis 17:15-27 AMP

Abram receives a name change and so does Sarai. Her new name is Sarah, his is Abraham. God promises to bless Abraham and to give him a son through her. Abraham falls on his face and laughs saying, " Shall a child be born to a man who is a hundred years old and Sarah who is ninety years old?" Abraham goes on to say to God, " Oh that Ishmael might live before You!"

Here we have Abraham interceding for his first-born son, and pleading, " God I wish that he would be your choice, I wish that he would be my heir, I wish that the covenant would be between you and him." God responds and says, " No, Sarah your wife will bear you a son and you shall call him Isaac. My covenant will be an everlasting covenant with him and his descendants after him." God tells Abraham, "As for Ishmael, I have heard you and listened to you. I have blessed Ishmael and will make him fruitful and greatly multiply him and I will make of him a great nation but my covenant is with Isaac whom Sarah will bear to you on this time next year."

Prayer is always in order. You may not receive the answer you are expecting, but you should still pray. Pray until God speaks to you like he spoke to Abraham concerning Ishmael, his firstborn son when he said, " I have heard you and listened." Don't pray one time and call it quits, be tenacious. Pursue after God in prayer. Pursue Him until you get His attention. Stay in pursuit until you receive the answer.

So God finishes speaking and Abraham does according to what the covenant contract between him and God requires.

"On the same day Abraham, Ishmael and all the servants of his household, including those born in the household or purchased with money, are circumcised." – Genesis 17:23

Intercession for the Wicked
As believers, it is also essential that we intercede for the wicked. Our prayers can cause God's hand to move on their behalf, and turn them from wickedness to righteousness.

"For I have known (chosen, acknowledged) him [as My own], so that he may teach and command his children and the sons of his house after him to keep the way of the Lord and to do what is just and righteous, so that the Lord may bring Abraham what He has promised him. And the Lord said, Because the shriek [of the sins] of Sodom and Gomorrah is great and their sin is exceedingly grievous, I will go down now and see whether they have done altogether [as vilely and wickedly] as is the cry of it which has come to Me; and if not, I will know. Now the [two] men turned from there and went toward

Sodom, but Abraham still stood before the Lord. And Abraham came close and said, Will You destroy the righteous (those upright and in right standing with God) together with the wicked? Suppose there are in the city fifty righteous; will You destroy the place and not spare it for [the sake of] the fifty righteous in it? Far be it from You to do such a thing—to slay the righteous with the wicked, so that the righteous fare as do the wicked! Far be it from You! Shall not the Judge of all the earth execute judgment and do righteously? And the Lord said, If I find in the city of Sodom fifty righteous (upright and in right standing with God), I will spare the whole place for their sake. Abraham answered, Behold now, I who am but dust and ashes have taken upon myself to speak to the Lord. If five of the fifty righteous should be lacking—will You destroy the whole city for lack of five? He said, If I find forty-five, I will not destroy it. And [Abraham] spoke to Him yet again, and said, Suppose [only] forty shall be found there. And He said, I will not do it for forty's sake. Then [Abraham] said to Him, Oh, let not the Lord be angry, and I will speak [again]. Suppose [only] thirty shall be found there. And He answered, I will not do it if I find thirty there. And [Abraham] said, Behold now, I have taken upon myself to speak [again] to the Lord. Suppose [only] twenty shall be found there. And [the Lord] replied, I will not destroy it for twenty's sake. And he said, Oh, let not the Lord be angry, and I will speak again only this once. Suppose ten [righteous people] shall be found there. And [the Lord] said, I will not destroy it for ten's sake. And the Lord went His way when He had finished speaking with Abraham, and Abraham returned to his place." - Genesis 18:16-33 AMPC

Just like Abraham, when God shares his thoughts with you concerning the wicked, you should not rejoice in their downfall, but instead you should intercede on their behalf. Intercessors should never desire death for the wicked. We should desire that God would extend unto them His hand of grace and mercy. Even Jesus, while on the cross, took time to pray to His father saying, "Father forgive them for they know not what they do." As an intercessor you should have a heart of mercy and compassion. If you don't have this, then work towards obtaining it.

"Blessed are those who hunger and thirst for righteousness, for they shall be filled." - Matthew 5:6 NKJV

Abraham offered prayers of intercession for Sodom and Gomorrah, not just his nephew Lot and his family. He literally interceded for everyone, the righteous as well as the unrighteous. We are not to judge, we are to pray. Intercessors your heart must be pure and untainted in order to pray effectively.

"Search me, O God, and know my heart; Try me, and know my anxieties;" - Psalms 139:23 NKJV

Ask God to search your heart and reveal anything that might keep your prayers from being answered.

Sodom's Destruction

The Lord releases hail and brimstone on Sodom and Gomorrah, but not before He allows Lot and his family to escape. Abraham's intercession is successful in staying the hand of destruction until his family makes it out safely.

Ishmael Prays

In Genesis 21:9-21, the Lord remembers and fulfills his promise to Sarah and Abraham. She that was once called barren receives strength at the set time God has chosen for her to give birth to the son of the promise. Per God's instruction, Isaac is circumcised on the eighth day. The child grows and is weaned by the age of three and Abraham holds a feast on the same day to celebrate. By now you would think that all would be well within the family, but it's not. Sarah comes upon Ishmael mocking Isaac, and she tells her husband to drive out the maid and her son because the maid's son will not be an heir with Isaac. I'm absolutely certain that Abraham didn't see this coming. They were all one big happy family. God had kept His word, and here was Isaac, the son of the promise, a reminder to all that God indeed is faithful even in your old age. Abraham is distressed about his son Ishmael. No he wasn't the promise, but he was his son, and Abraham loved him.

Abraham taught Ishmael about prayer and communion with God. He and Ishmael had great father and son times. Wherever you saw Abraham, Ishmael was never far behind. He was his father's shadow, and he was growing by leaps and bounds, and getting taller everyday. Abraham asked God how he could drive them out, and God spoke saying, "It's alright. Don't let this matter with Hagar and Ishmael distress you. I want you to do whatever Sarah asks you, but know this one thing, your descendants will be named through Isaac. I haven't forgotten about Ishmael. I will make of him a great nation because he is your son."

Abraham does as Sarah suggests and rising up early the next morning he gives Hagar bread and water and sends her and Ishmael away. They leave from under the protection of Abraham's house, and Hagar becomes lost. Later she and Ishmael are found wandering around in the wilderness of Beersheba. After consuming all of the water Abraham had given them, Hagar abandons her son under a bush and sits a bow shot away from him saying, "Do not let me see my son die." She begins to weep. God hears the voice of Ishmael, the son of Abraham, because God is acquainted with him. God has not forgotten the time Abraham and Ishmael spent in his presence, quality time, not rushed or hurried, but sacred and holy time. Hagar is in distress because she can no longer provide for him. Ishmael remembers the prayers that he and Abraham prayed as they knelt beside the altar and called upon the name of the Lord. He remembers praying for strength in weak moments and for sustenance. He has been instructed by his father on how to pray, so he utilizes every tool he has been given. His mother's cries have almost become unbearable until he hears a voice from heaven calling her name, asking her what is troubling her and telling her not to be afraid because God has heard Ishmael's prayers from where he was resting. The voice from heaven tells her, "Get up and help your son up. Hold him by his hand for I am making him a great nation."

    God then opens her eyes and she sees a well of water. Provision has been made, so she goes and fills up an empty skin with water and gives it to Ishmael to drink. Abraham's teaching had paid off. Ishmael recalls his father saying, "My son, after you have prayed unto God, rest in the fact that by faith he has heard your prayers, has seen your tears and will answer in his timing." Ishmael, much like his father Abraham, is tenacious even in the midst of a hard place. He had learned the secret, that if you call upon the name of the Lord God from a pure heart, He will come to your aid and He will rescue you.

What an awesome secret to have in your arsenal! What if Ishmael had given up? What if he had stopped praying? God told his mother that he had heard her son's prayers, which tells me you are never too young to call on the name of the Lord God.

"But He said, "Leave the children alone, and do not forbid them from coming to Me; for the kingdom of heaven belongs to such as these."" - Matthew 19:14 AMP

God heard Ishmael's voice as he cried out to him. His age did not hinder his prayers from being heard or answered. Just the same, it is never too early to teach your child to pray. Just as Abraham taught Ishmael, you too should teach your children how to be skillful in intercession. When you go into your prayer closet, take your child with you. Allow them to watch you as you enter into the presence of the Lord God, so that they might learn to do the same.

"Train up a child in the way he should go [teaching him to seek God's wisdom and will for his abilities and talents], Even when he is old he will not depart from it." - Proverbs 22:6 AMP

Isaac Offers Prayers of Intercession for Rebekah

"Isaac was forty years old when he married Rebekah, the daughter of Bethuel the Aramean (Syrian) of Paddan-aram, the sister of Laban the Aramean. Isaac prayed to the Lord for his wife, because she was unable to conceive children; and the LORD granted his prayer and Rebekah his wife conceived [twins]." - Genesis 25:20-21 AMP

Three years after the death of his mother, Isaac married Rebekah. Because of Rebekah's inability to conceive, Isaac interceded for her. Isaac's request was granted and Rebekah conceived twins.

Have you ever had to wait patiently on a promise? It may have seemed like your prayers had not been heard, but like Isaac you mounted an offensive in prayer and you interceded until God not only listened, but He also responded by giving you your heart's desire. God is still answering prayers, just as he answered Isaac's prayer on behalf of Rebekah. Because of Isaac's intercession, the barren womb received strength to conceive seed, and God didn't just give Rebekah one child, she received a double harvest.

Rebekah Asks Why

"But the children struggled together within her [kicking and shoving one another]; and she said "If it is so [that the LORD has heard our prayer], why then am I this way?" So she went to inquire of the LORD [praying for an answer]. The LORD said to her, " [The founders of] two nations are in your womb; And the separation of two nations has begun in your body; The one people shall be stronger than the other; And the older shall serve the younger."" - Genesis 25:22-23 AMP

As the twins struggle within her, Rebekah questions why she is experiencing so much distress, and offers prayers of supplication to God. God responds and lets her know that the reason for her distress is because there are two nations in her womb.

Like Rebekah, the struggle on the inside of you may be very real, but God has a purpose for it all. All things are working together for your good. Keep a winning attitude as the war continues to rage; because hands down you will win!

Isaac Offers Prayers to the Lord

"Then he went up from there to Beersheba. The LORD appeared to him the same night and said, " I am the God of Abraham your father; Do not be afraid, for I am with you. I will bless and favor you, and multiply your descendants, For the sake of My servant Abraham." So Isaac built an altar there and called on the name of the LORD [in prayer]. He pitched his tent there; and there Isaac's servants dug a well."
- Genesis 26:23-25 AMP

In this passage of scripture, God speaks to Isaac in a dream and assures him that the covenant he made with his father, still stands and applies to him.

As believers and intercessors it is important to know that God has never broken a covenant, nor will he ever. He believes in keeping His word. Despite everything that comes to try your patience, when God comes, He brings a word of encouragement, and a word to strengthen your flanks. He says to you, just as he said to Isaac, " Do not be afraid for I am with you and will bless you, favor you and multiply your descendants." Receive this word on today.

Isaac Offers Prayers of Blessings On Jacob

"So he came and kissed him; and Isaac smelled his clothing and blessed him and said, " The scent of my son [Esau] is like the aroma of a field which the LORD has blessed; Now may God give you of the dew of heaven [to water your land], And of the fatness (fertility) of the earth, And an abundance of grain and new wine; May people serve you, And nations bow down to you. May those who curse you be cursed, And may those who bless you be blessed." Now as soon as Isaac had finished blessing Jacob, and Jacob had scarcely left the presence of Isaac his father, Esau his brother came in from his hunting."

- Genesis 27:27-30 AMP

Jacob resorted to trickery to receive the blessing intended for Esau. As intercessors may you never resort to this level to obtain anything. It is not worth it. In the end it will definitely cause more harm than good. Rebekah and Jacob's plot ultimately fractured their family, splitting it down the middle. So be mindful of what you allow your flesh to lead you into. Lies and trickery are not of God. Neither is being manipulative or controlling.

As intercessors it is essential that we do a consistent heart check to ensure we are not operating from this place. If you find that you are operating in any of these things, petition God for a clean heart and ask that He renew the right spirit within you.

Isaac Offers Another Prayer of Blessings On Jacob

"So Isaac called Jacob and blessed him and charged him, and said to him, " You shall not marry one of the women of Canaan. Arise, go to Paddan-aram, to the house of Bethuel your mother's father; and take from there as a wife for yourself

one of the daughters of Laban your mother's brother. May God Almighty bless you and make you fruitful and multiply you, so that you may become a [great] company of peoples. May He also give the blessing of Abraham to you and your descendants with you, that you may inherit the [promised] land of your sojournings, which He gave to Abraham."''

- Genesis 28:1-4 AMP

As an intercessor, it is important to train your children in the ways of the Lord, so that when the time presents itself you can give them instructions concerning dating and marriage. Do I believe in dating? Yes, I do. How can you expect to know someone if you don't date? But do it the Lord's way, not your way. God has a vested interest in marriage. So whether you are seeking Him for yourself or for your child, ask God for wisdom in this area.

Leah's Prayers of Supplication Are Answered

" *God listened and answered [the prayer of] Leah, and she conceived and gave birth to a fifth son for Jacob. Then Leah said, " God has given me my reward because I have given my maid to my husband." So she named him Issachar. Leah conceived again and gave birth to a sixth son for Jacob. Then Leah said, " God has endowed me with a good [marriage] gift [for my husband]; now he will live with me [regarding me with honor as his wife], because I have given birth to six sons." So she named him Zebulun. Afterward she gave birth to a daughter and named her Dinah."* - Genesis 30:17-21 AMP

The Lord listened to the prayers of supplication by Leah, and he opened her womb so that she could conceive. Intercessor you may find yourself in an undesirable situation, but prayer is still in order. Like Leah, pray until

God responds. Your situation may be different than Leah's, but God is still concerned about you, so continue to pray until God moves on your behalf.

Rachel's Prayers of Supplication Are Remembered by God

"Then God remembered [the prayers of] Rachel, and God thought of her and opened her womb [so that she would conceive]. So she conceived and gave birth to a son; and she said, " God has taken away my disgrace and humiliation." She named him Joseph (may He add) and said, " May the LORD add to me another son."" - Genesis 30:22-24 AMP

God remembers the prayers of supplication prayed by Rachel during her years of barrenness, so He opens her womb and she conceives and gives birth to a son.
   Intercessor, God is fair and just. He loves us all the same. Your petitions have gone before Him just like Rachel's, and to you it seems like He is taking a very long time to respond. You may even be saying to yourself, "I've been waiting and waiting, when is He going to respond." Be encouraged, in due time God will move on your behalf.

Laban Offers Prayers of Blessings

"Early in the morning Laban got up and kissed his grandchildren and his daughters [goodbye] and pronounced a blessing [asking God's favor] on them. Then Laban left and returned home." - Genesis 31:55 AMP

In this passage it was not Laban's intent to bless them, but when God says he will make your enemies to be at peace with you, this is exactly what he means. Laban had no choice but to fall in line with the will of God, and speak a blessing over them. It was God ordained intercession. Intercessors, the enemy may contemplate harming you, but God can and will make them bless you.

Jacob Offers Prayers of Supplication & Intercession

"Jacob said, " O God of my father Abraham and God of my father Isaac, the LORD, who said to me, 'Return to your country and to your people, and I will make you prosper,' I am unworthy of all the lovingkindness and compassion and of all the faithfulness which You have shown to Your servant. With only my staff [long ago] I crossed over this Jordan, and now I have become [blessed and increased into these] two groups [of people]. Save me, please, from the hand of my brother, from the hand of Esau; for I fear him, that he will come and attack me and the mothers with the children. And You [LORD] said, ' I will certainly make you prosper and make your descendants as [numerous as] the sand of the sea, which is too great to be counted."" - Genesis 32:9-12 AMP

Just like Jacob you may be facing a situation that may me potentially harmful to you and others. Ask the Lord to save you from whomever and whatever is attempting to come against you. Ask God to keep you safe from all hurt, harm and danger; and believe that He hears and will answer accordingly.

Israel Offers Prayers of Blessings Over Joseph

"Then Joseph took them both, Ephraim with his right hand towards Israel's left, and Manasseh with his left hand toward Israel's right, and brought them close to him. But Israel reached out his right hand and laid it on the head of Ephraim, who was the younger, and his left hand on Manasseh's head; crossing his hands [intentionally], even though Manasseh was the firstborn. Then Jacob (Israel) blessed Joseph, and said, " The God before whom my fathers Abraham and Isaac walked [in faithful obedience], The God who has been my Shepherd [leading and caring for me] all my life to this day, The Angel [that is, the LORD Himself] who has redeemed me [continually] from all evil, Bless the boys; And may my name live on in them [may they be worthy of having their names linked with mine], And the names of my fathers Abraham and Isaac; And may they grow into a [great] multitude in the midst of the earth."" - Genesis 48:13-16 AMP

Joseph arrives at the bedside of his father Jacob, and Jacob pronounces a blessing over him. As intercessors we too have the power to bestow blessings upon our children and our children's children. What an awesome example we have in Jacob who refused to die before leaving a blessing behind. Release that blessing intercessor. You have the right to do it. Don't allow the enemy to stop you. May all of those you bless, walk in God's favor.

Chapter Two

The Book of Exodus

A prayer of lament is a tool that God's people use to navigate pain and suffering. Lamenting is vital for the people of God because it allows us to petition God to deliver us from distress, suffering and pain. A prayer of lament is designed to persuade God on behalf of the sufferer.

The Lamentation of the People Is Seen and Heard

"Now it happened after a long time [about forty years] that the king of Egypt died. And the children of Israel (Jacob) groaned and sighed because of the bondage, and they cried out. And their cry for help because of their bondage ascended to God. So God heard their groaning and God remembered His covenant with Abraham, Isaac, and Jacob (Israel). God saw the sons of Israel, and God took notice [of them] and was concerned about them [knowing all, understanding all, remembering all]."
                                       - Exodus 2:23-25 AMP

Forty years have now passed and the king of Egypt that sought to kill Moses has died and the children of Israel, because of their suffering at the hands of the taskmasters and those that have rule over them, have begun to offer up petitions to the Lord for his divine intervention. As we see in this text, prayers of lament are being prayed in order to deal with the bondage that they are in. The text tells us that not only is God listening, but now, as only a loving father would do, He remembers the covenant promises that he made with His servants- Abraham, Isaac and Jacob. Unbeknownst to the Israelites, God is about to do something about the problem at hand using a deliverer by the name of Moses, from the tribe of Levi.

Prayers of lament were offered up to God by the children of Israel because of the hardships they endured. There will be times in your life, whether it be loss of a job, the death of a loved one, or a family member dealing with sickness or a life threatening illness, that you too will need to offer up a prayer of lament. Tests, trials and tribulations will come to us all because it is the way of life and there are some things that we must face head on. When you encounter these moments with groaning and tears, and prayers that cannot be uttered, just know that God understands every groan and He will wipe away all of your tears.

"And He will wipe away every tear from their eyes; and there will no longer be death; there will no longer be sorrow and anguish, or crying, or pain; for the former order of things has passed away." - Revelation 2:14 AMP

The first forty years of Moses' life is spent in Egypt in the house of Pharaoh. Now at the ripe age of eighty, we find Moses, the son-in-law of Jethro, the priest of Midian, tending to his father-in-law's flock. Moses leads the herd of sheep to the west side of the wilderness where the mountain of God is located. The occupation of shepherd might have been repulsive to the Egyptians, but Moses had forty years in this job, which taught him to be caring and how to submit and humble himself. There were no accolades in the wilderness, no servants to meet his needs, and no one bowed when he entered a room. This was a transforming and life altering time for Moses. The job of shepherd was about to open a new door to Moses as the deliverer of Israel.

While Moses is tending to the flock, an angel of the Lord appears to him in a bush that burned with fire but did not wither away. Moses says to himself, "Let me leave the flock where they are, and investigate this great thing that is happening right before my very eyes." When the Lord saw that he had Moses' full attention, He calls his name from the bush. He says, "Moses." Moses replies, "Here I am." Then God said, "Don't come any closer. Remove your sandals because the ground that you are on is holy ground." God begins his introduction to Moses by introducing himself as the God of his father, the God of Abraham, the God of Issac and the God of Jacob. Moses then hides his face because he is afraid to look at God.

The Lord continues speaking to Moses and says, "I want you to know that I have seen with my own eyes the oppression that my people are facing in Egypt, and their prayers of lamentation have not gone unnoticed. I see the sin of the taskmasters and I understand their sorrows. So I have come down to deliver them out of the hand of their adversaries the Egyptians and I will bring them out of that land and place them in a land where milk and honey flows freely. I promised their father and my friend Abraham that the land of the Canaanites, the Hittites, the Amorites, the Perizzites, the Hivites, and the Jebusites would be their portion. Now behold Moses, the cry of the children of Israel has come to me and I have seen how they are oppressed by the Egyptians."

The Assignment Explained

In Exodus 3:10-22, we see God beginning to answer the prayers of the Israelites. God is preparing Moses, and gives him clear instructions on where he is to go, what he is to do, who he is to bring with him, and what he is to say when he approaches Pharaoh about freeing the Israelites from captivity. He even forewarns him about the hardness of Pharaoh's heart, and how he will initially refuse to let them go, but in the end God will prevail.

Power Given For the Task Ahead

Read Exodus 4:1-13 AMP

The fourth chapter of Exodus begins with Moses doubting his abilities to speak clearly enough, so that people would listen to him. Moses begins tossing out scenarios to God, "What if they say to me, "You have not seen God, how do we know if what you are saying is the truth?"" So God asks Moses, "What is that in your hand?" Moses replies, "It's a rod." God said, "Cast it down on the ground. Moses does as instructed and the rod that he has used on many occasions to shepherd the flock and to lean upon as he walked, has now turned into a serpent right before his very eyes. Moses becomes so afraid that he runs away.

    The Lord tells Moses to take up the serpent by the tail and when he does the serpent turns into a rod. God says, "Moses perform this sign in front of the elders of Israel. This sign will cause them to believe that I have sent you on this assignment." God then instructs Moses to put his hand into the chest area of his robe, so Moses places his hand inside of his robe and as he removes his hand, it is leprous, and as white as snow. God says, "Put it into your robe again." This time when he removes it, his hand is whole and complete, just like the other hand. God says to Moses, "If they will not believe the first sign, perhaps they will believe this one. Moses there will be many present in your midst that will not believe either sign that you perform, so here is what I want you to do. I want you to take water from the Nile in the presence of all the elders, pour the water upon the dry ground and once this is done the water will turn into blood."

Then Moses said to the Lord, "Lord, please, I don't want to bring shame upon you. I have a speech problem. I can't form my words like everyone else. I'm a little bit shy. From the moment you called to me from the burning bush, until now, I have not been able to wrap my mind around this assignment. I've practiced what you want me to say, but it never seems to come out right." God responds, "Who do you think made man's mouth to speak, or the deaf, or mute, or those that are blind? I want you to stop with all of the excuses. Don't doubt what I can do through you, just obey me and go and I will be with your mouth and I'll be your teacher." Moses says, "I hear what you're saying, but please hear my petition and give this part of the assignment to someone else."

Even when an assignment looks too big for us, we have to trust that God knows what is on the inside of us because he placed it there. Moses was busy telling God everything about himself- from I can't speak, to I'm a little slow in this area or I'm not too skilled in that area, but God already knew what Moses was capable of doing. He created him and our creator God knows all. So when we are sent on an assignment like Moses and we don't feel qualified to do the job, guess what, he already qualified you, so offer your petitions to God like Moses, and push forward. Let God know about all of your concerns and insecurities, and he will address each and everyone of them.

Round One With Pharaoh

Read Exodus 5:1-23 AMP

When Moses initially approaches Pharaoh about freeing the Israelites, instead of releasing them, he intensifies their labor and treats them even more harshly. Because of this, the Israelites turn on Moses. Moses, being an intercessor, begins to cry out to God on their behalf. The Israelites had been oppressed for over four hundred years, but when this new challenge was thrust upon them they felt defeated and let down by God. They could not see the hand of God moving on their behalf, but just because they couldn't see it in the natural, didn't mean God was not working behind the scenes. God had sent Moses and Aaron to remind them that he was concerned about their well-being. They had seen with their own eyes what God was capable of doing. They saw His mighty acts, but when life showed up in a way they weren't expecting, the hope they had walked straight out the door.

God Answers and Makes Promises

Read Exodus 6:1-13 AMP

In Exodus 5 we find Moses in intercession, trying to understand why God has sent him on such a task that has resulted in more harm and oppression to the children of Israel. Moses tells God that he has done nothing at all to rescue the people. The Lord responds, "You are about to witness what I am about to bring upon Pharaoh. With force he will let my people go and with great force he will drive them out of his land." As God continues to speak to Moses, He reinforces his sovereignty by saying, "I am the

Lord. I appeared to Abraham, Issac and Jacob as God Almighty, but by my name, Lord, they didn't know me by. I established my covenant with them. I promised to give them the land of Canaan, the land they were strangers in. Do not think that I have not heard their prayers of lament as well as every petition that has come up before me because of the sufferings and pain that they have endured; and I have not forgotten the covenant that I made with Abraham, Isaac and Jacob (Israel). Tell them that I remember it like it was yesterday. Tell the children of Israel that I am the Lord and that the burden that the Egyptians have you under, you are about to escape from and walk into your freedom. I am redeeming you and I have a plan in motion to rescue you with my mighty arm and with my acts of judgment, which will be performed. I am your God and I have taken you as my people, and you will know that I have purchased you and brought you from under the Egyptian's burden."

    Moses returns to the people with the message from the Lord, but they turn a deaf ear because they are impatient and because of the cruelty that had been heaped upon them.

    The Lord says to Moses, "I want you to go and tell Pharaoh, King of Egypt, to allow my children to leave his land." Moses responds, "But my Lord, my own people, the ones that you have sent me to, don't listen to me, so please tell me why should Pharaoh? I told you before we got to this point that I am unskilled in matters like these." The Lord speaks to both Moses and Aaron and commands them concerning the children of Israel and Pharaoh king of Egypt, to bring his people out of the land of bondage.

Can't Stop, Don't Stop

Intercessors your prayers are needed. You must continue to cry out in intercession just as Moses cried out for the people of Israel. Even when you feel like you are in a losing battle, pray intercessors pray. Take a deep breath, square your shoulders and get back in there. You have come to far to give up. Your city needs you! Your community needs you! Your nation needs your intercession! Even if the devil speaks in your ear telling you that you don't have anything else to give, know that he is a liar and continue to push in prayer. Don't stop praying. You have family that are thriving and existing on the prayers that you pray. Just as Moses interceded for the people and they were sustained because of his prayers, know that your prayers are also sustaining someone.

Pharaoh Requests Prayer
'
"Then Pharaoh called for Moses and Aaron and said, "Plead with the LORD that He may take away the frogs from me and my people; and I will let the people go, so that they may sacrifice to the LORD." And Moses said to Pharaoh, "I am entirely at your service: when shall I plead [with the Lord] for you and your servants and your people, so that the frogs may leave you and your houses and remain only in the Nile?" Then Pharaoh said, " Tomorrow." Moses replied, " May it be as you say, so that you may know [without any doubt] and acknowledge that there is no one like the LORD our God. The frogs will leave you and your houses and leave your servants and your people; they will remain only in the Nile." So Moses and Aaron left Pharaoh, and Moses cried out to the LORD [as he had agreed to do] concerning the frogs which God had inflicted on Pharaoh. The LORD did as Moses asked, and the frogs died out of the houses, out of the courtyards and villages,

and out of the fields. So they piled them up in heaps, and the land was detestable and stank. But when Pharaoh saw that there was [temporary] relief, he hardened his heart and would not listen or pay attention to them, just as the LORD had said."
- Exodus 8:8-15 AMP

Pharaoh requests prayer from Moses concerning the pestilence of frogs that had been released upon the Egyptians by God. Once Moses' prayer of intercession is answered, Pharaoh resorts back to his old ways. There will be many people in your life that will ask you to pray for them. It may be your supervisor or the owner of the company that you work for, it could even be a leader that you know whose life is not clean, intercessors pray and don't pass judgment.

"First of all, then, I urge that petitions (specific requests), prayers, intercessions (prayers for others) and thanksgivings be offered on behalf of all people, for kings and all who are in [positions of] high authority, so that we may live a peaceful and quiet life in all godliness and dignity."
- 1 Timothy 2:1-2 AMP

Moses could have gotten an attitude with Pharaoh, but he didn't because God had already made it very clear that he was going to harden Pharaoh's heart. As an intercessor here is what you need to do... "Pray without ceasing (1 Thessalonians 5:17 NKJV)."

You may say to yourself that they are wicked and don't deserve my prayers, but intercessor you were once wicked but through the intercession of someone else, God listened and gave you a mind to come out of sin. All God needs is a willing vessel, one that doesn't mind laying a foundation of prayer. You may be saying I pray and I pray, but they are still doing wrong and it looks like the more I pray the worst off they become. Listen very carefully, God has something to say, "Do not fret because of evildoers, Nor be envious of the workers of iniquity (Psalms 37:1 NKJV)."

Pharaoh requested prayer from Moses on three different occasions, and every time God answered, Pharaoh returned to his old ways. As an intercessor it is your job to pray, but it is God's job to answer and deal with the hearts of men. Allow God to answer and move in His timing, just keep seeking Him.

Placing Blame

"As Pharaoh approached, the Israelites looked up and saw the Egyptians marching after them, and they were very frightened; so the Israelites cried out to the LORD. Then they said to Moses, "Is it because there are no graves in Egypt that you have taken us away to die in the wilderness? What is this that you have done to us by bringing us out of Egypt? Did we not say to you in Egypt, 'Leave us alone; let us serve the Egyptians?' For it would have been better for us to serve the Egyptians [as slaves] than to die in the wilderness.""
- Exodus 14:10-12 AMP

While camped by the Red Sea, the children of Israel see their former master approaching and he's not alone. There are numerous chariots and riders heading their way. It can't be a good thing that he has come, so the people are frightened, lift up their voices like one man and cry out and lift up prayers of supplication unto the Lord. Prayers of supplication to the Lord in times of trouble was definitely the right thing to do; and asking for deliverance in a situation where they were between a rock and a hard place was also the right thing to do. But when God doesn't respond to them in the way they think he should, the miracles that God performed in Egypt against Pharaoh, his servants and his people are momentarily forgotten. Now it's time to cast blame so they say to Moses, "Weren't there enough graves in Egypt? Why would you bring us here to this barren place to die? Why did you bring us out here? While we were in Egypt didn't we say to you to let us be, let us serve the Egyptians? We should have stayed in Egypt and died as slaves rather than making this journey into the wilderness where we will surely perish."

"There is a way that seems right to a man, But its end is the way of death." -Proverbs 14:12 NKJV

It's amazing how the people offered up prayers of supplication, but in the same breath when it seemed like there was no answer forthcoming, they began to place blame on their leader, Moses. You cannot offer prayers of supplication and place blame at the same time. A double-minded man is unstable in all his ways and the Israelites were definitely double-minded.

Intercessors if you are double-minded you cannot be effective for the kingdom of God. You can't pray effectively and have doubt in your heart too.

"Being a double-minded man, unstable and restless in all his ways [in everything he thinks, feels, or decides]."
- James 1:8 AMP

Come out of agreement with being double minded the word of God asks this question, "Can two walk together, unless they are agreed (Amos 3:3 NJKV)?"

You and God have to be on the same page. Blaming him because he didn't give you what you wanted when you asked for it is very childish and very petty. Grow up intercessors and own up to where you really are. Be like the father in Mark 9:24, "Immediately the father of the child cried out and said with tears, "Lord, I believe; help my unbelief!"" Either you believe God or you don't.

Moses and the People Offer Praise and Thanksgiving

In Exodus 15:1-21, God has kept His word as he always does, and has delivered his people out of the hands of their adversaries. The song we see in this scripture is very detailed and is a verbal declaration of God's awesome might and power.

Though this song is one of praise and thanksgiving, it is also a weapon. Psalm 150:6 says, "Let everything that has breath praise the Lord!"

Singing is a God given weapon that has been given to every believer. Prayers of praise and thanksgiving bring us closer to God and while you are offering unto him the sacrifice of praise it dismantles unbelief and pushes the adversary back. The devil does not want you to praise the Lord. Your prayers of praise and thanksgiving are awesome weapons to have. Learn to utilize them daily.

Even as Moses and the people sang praises and offered thanksgiving to the Lord, so should you. When God brings you out of a test with victory, give him some praise! When you have interceded for someone and God grants them a miracle, sing praises to the Lord Most High.

"I will praise the name of God with a song, And will magnify Him with thanksgiving." – Psalms 69:30 NKJV

Don't wait until God answers your prayers to sing to Him. Do it while you are waiting on the manifestation of the prayer. Break out in praise and thanksgiving because He is deserving of all honor and praise.

Water Is Provided By the Lord

"Then Moses led Israel from the Red Sea, and they went into the Wilderness of Shur; they went [a distance of] three days (about thirty-three miles) in the wilderness and found no water. Then they came to Marah, but they could not drink its waters because they were bitter; therefore it was named Marah (bitter). The people [grew discontented and] grumbled at Moses, saying, "What are we going to drink?" Then he cried to the LORD [for help], and the LORD showed him a tree, [a branch of] which he threw into the waters, and the waters became sweet. There the LORD made a statute and an ordinance for them, and there He tested them, saying, "If you will diligently listen and pay attention to the voice of the LORD your God, and do what is right in His sight, and listen to His commandments, and keep [foremost in your thoughts and actively obey] all His precepts and statutes, then I will not put on you any of the diseases which I have put on the Egyptians; for I am the LORD who heals you." Then the children of Israel came to Elim where there were twelve springs of water and seventy date palms, and they camped there beside the waters."
- Exodus 15:22-27 AMP

Moses, under the direction of the Lord, has led the people from the Red Sea into the wilderness. After about three days or 33 miles in the wilderness, they find no water. As they came to Marah, they found water but they could not drink it because it was bitter; so they named it Marah, which means bitter. The people begin to grumble and complain to Moses asking, "What are we going to drink?"

Moses offers up prayers of intercession concerning this situation and the Lord answers by showing him a tree and instructing him to throw it into the water. Upon doing this, the water becomes drinkable.

In Exodus 15, we see Moses once again having to deal with the murmuring and complaining of the people. Intercessors, there will be people around you who will murmur and complain over the smallest thing, God brought me out here to hurt me, God doesn't really care about me, and on and on and on. Intercessors don't allow frustration to come into play. Just intercede because that is what you have been called to do. Like Moses, cry out for them and when they mess up again cry out once more. Moses is a great example of a powerful intercessor. He was dedicated and diligent concerning the task at hand, just as you should be.

Moses' Intercession

Read Exodus 32:7-14 AMP

While on the mount God tells Moses to go down at once because your people, who you brought out of Egypt, have turned away quickly from what they promised. God begins telling Moses everything that the people had done while he was on the mount. He then says, "Look I understand this people very well. I see their sin and they are rebellious towards me, leave me alone and don't intercede for them because I want to destroy them; and once my anger has abated I'll make of your descendants a great nation." Moses, being the intercessor that he is, begins offering up prayers in the spirit. Praying the will of God in this manner, he makes an appeal to God's loving nature by questioning him in regards to what he wants to do. Moses asks God, "Why are you so angry at your people whom you brought out of Egypt with signs and wonders? Now you know once you slay them the Egyptians are going to say that your intentions towards them were evil all the time and that the reason you did it was to kill them in the mountains."

Moses continues his intercession for the people by asking God to turn his anger away and to change his mind about destroying them. Moses pushes his petition forward by reminding God about the promises that he had made to Abraham, Isaac and Jacob. You swore by yourself and said to them that you would multiply their descendants as the stars of heaven and that all the land was to be inherited by them." So the Lord changes his mind concerning harming his people.

""God is not a man, that He should lie, Nor a son of man, that He should repent. Has He said, and will He not do it? Or has He spoken and will He not make it good and fulfill it?"

-Numbers 23:19 AMP

Moses Intercedes Once Again

"Then the next day Moses said to the people, "You have committed a great sin. Now I will go up to the LORD; perhaps I can make atonement for your sin." So Moses returned to the LORD, and said, "Oh, these people have committed a great sin [against You], and have made themselves a god of gold. Yet now, if You will, forgive their sin--and if not, please blot me out of Your book which You have written (kill me)!" But the LORD said to Moses, "Whoever has sinned against Me, I will blot him out of My book [not you]. But now go, lead the people [to the place] where I have told you. Behold, My Angel shall go before you; nevertheless, in the day when I punish, I will punish them for their sin!" So the LORD struck the people with a plague,

because of what they had done with the calf which Aaron had made [for them]." - Exodus 32:30-35 AMP

The people have sinned against God once again, and now we see Moses interceding on their behalf yet again. What God had done for them in freeing them from captivity and providing for them in the wilderness did not seem to matter. Though they were no longer in Egypt, Egypt ands its practices were still in them. Because of this, Moses had to consistently stay in the face of God on their behalf.

    As I mentioned before, the job of the intercessor is not one for the faint of heart. It is for those that believe they are capable and qualified to carry out the assignment at hand. Put yourself in Moses's shoes. We see him handling every murmur and complaint, as well as doubt and unbelief that the people had. He dealt with all of it in intercession, just as we should. The things that Moses faced on a daily, weekly, monthly or yearly basis is nothing new any of us. I'm sure you have had to deal with family members that don't believe fully in the God that you serve, but once something goes terribly wrong who do they call, text, or iMessage, the intercessor of course. People's lives hang in the balance on a daily basis and you are the mediator between them and God. Intercede and speak life over them, not death. Your words have power and authority, use what He has given to you. Open your mouth wide and pray. Stay the course. Don't throw in the towel. As the children of Israel needed the intercession of Moses, your intercession is needed in the earth realm as well.

Chapter Three

The Book of Numbers

Aaron's Prayer of Blessing Over Israel

"Then the LORD spoke to Moses, saying, "Speak to Aaron and his sons, saying, 'This is the way you shall bless the Israelites. Say to them: The LORD bless you, and keep you [protect you, sustain you, and guard you]; The LORD make His face shine upon you [with favor], And be gracious to you [surrounding you with lovingkindness]; The LORD lift up His countenance (face) upon you [with divine approval], And give you peace [a tranquil heart and life].' So Aaron and his sons shall put My name upon the children of Israel, and I will bless them.'"

-Numbers 6:22-27 AMP

    Moses was instructed by God to speak to Aaron and to his sons, and to tell them that they were to bless the children of Israel in this manner. They were to pronounce a prayer of blessings over them; and the prayer of blessings would consist of God's favor being placed upon them as well as his protection, his sustaining power, his guidance and his loving kindness. The Lord's face would also always be upon them with approval and he would give them his shalom, so the name of God would be placed upon them and they would carry his blessings.

    Aaron and his sons were instructed by God through Moses to bless the children of Israel. It is important that our spiritual leaders release over the people in their congregations a blessing of God's favor and protection. It is also very important for intercessors that have been called to intercede on behalf of various cities and states, as well as our nation, to speak a prayer of blessing of God's favor and his protection. On the news we see countless stories of war, upheaval, murder and chaos, but you have a word in your mouth to counter this. Pronounce a blessing over the region that you reside in, intercessor. This is so needful in the hour in which we are living.

Moses' Declaration of Faith

"So they set out from the mountain of the LORD (Sinai) three days' journey; and the ark of the covenant of the LORD went in front of them during the three days' journey to seek out a resting place for them. The cloud of the LORD was over them by day when they set out from the camp. Whenever the ark set out, Moses said, "Rise up, O LORD! Let Your enemies be scattered; And let those who hate You flee before You." And when the ark rested, Moses said, "Return, O LORD, To the myriad (many) thousands of Israel." -Numbers 10:33-36 AMP

The Israelites going out and coming in serves as an example to us that we should begin and end every day's journey and every day's work with prayer. Moses's prayer when the ark moved forward was, *"Rise up, and let thine enemies be scattered."*

Moses Intercedes On the People's Behalf

"The LORD said to Moses, "How long will these people treat me disrespectfully and reject Me? And how long will they not believe in Me, despite all the [miraculous] signs which I have performed among them? I will strike them with the pestilence (plague) and dispossess them, and will make you into a nation greater and mightier than they." But Moses said to the LORD,

"Then the Egyptians will hear of it, for by Your strength You brought up these people from among them, and they will tell it to the inhabitants of this land. They have heard that You, LORD, are among these people [of Israel], that You, LORD, are seen face to face, while Your cloud stands over them; and that You go before them in a pillar of cloud by day and in a pillar of fire by night. Now if You kill these people as one man, then the nations (Gentiles) that have heard of Your fame will say, 'Because the LORD was not able to bring these people into the land which He promised to give them, therefore He slaughtered them in the wilderness.' But now, please, let the power of the Lord be great, just as You have declared, saying, 'The LORD is slow to anger, and abundant in lovingkindness, forgiving wickedness and transgression; but He will by no means clear the guilty, visiting (avenging) the wickedness and guilt of the fathers on the children, to the third and fourth generations [that is, calling the children to account for the sins of their fathers].' Please pardon the wickedness and guilt of these people according to the greatness of Your lovingkindness, just as You have forgiven these people, from Egypt even until now."
                                        -Numbers 14:11-19AMP

In this passage, Moses is teaching all intercessors something and that very valuable lesson is this, intercession for others, whether you know them or not, is needed daily.

God wanted to do away with the children of Israel and start from scratch, but an intercessor like Moses went to God on behalf of the murmuring and complaining children of Israel and began to shift God's mindset from killing off everyone to a mindset of forgiveness and mercy. That's what intercessors are called to do. We are to stand in the gap for all people. Yes, even those who murmur, complain and have no faith.

"So I sought for a man among them who would make a wall, and stand in the gap before Me on behalf of the land, that I should not destroy it; but I found no one."
- Ezekiel 22:30 NKJV

God is looking for you intercessor. Can you be found? Are you willing to be used by Him? Are you willing to say here I am Lord, give me the assignment and I will pray?

In the words of my spiritual mother, Prophetess Jacqueline Rhymes, "Intercessors you are the first line of defense. You must stand in the gap. You must pray. You don't have the luxury of throwing in the towel because your intercession is needful."

The Lord Pardons and A Death Sentence Is Handed Down

Read Numbers 14:20-38 AMP

Following Numbers 14, we see a rebellion led by Korah. In response to the rebellion, Moses and Aaron make intercession to God, but ultimately God's response to their intercession is to spare everyone except Korah and the men that had rebelled by rising up against Moses and Aaron.

When you are doing what God has commanded you to do, look for opposition. Opposition may take the form of jealousy, envy, strife, hatred and the list goes on and on. But know this one thing, God will deal with it. He is the God that sees and knows all and your intercession has not and will not go unnoticed.

The Lord Pardons and A Death Sentence Is Handed Down

The people once again begin to murmur and complain, so God instructs Moses to gather the people, take his rod and speak to the rock so that fresh water could sprout from it. Moses, in his anger and frustration, strikes the rock twice with his rod, and in doing so disobeys and dishonors God. Ultimately, his anger and lapse in judgment causes him to miss the Promised Land. He had led the people out of Egypt and in the wilderness, but he himself would be unable to enter the Promised Land.

Intercessors know this one thing. Be careful of what you allow to be released from your mouth. Don't ever allow a moment to become so heated that you forget who and what you have been called to do. Not being mindful of this will cause you to run the risk of forfeiting what God has in store for you. The words that you speak can cause you to forfeit what God has planned for you and can definitely delay your blessing.

"There is a way that seems right to a man, But its end is the way of death." -Proverbs 14:12 NKJV

The People Ask Moses to Intercede For Them

"Then the LORD sent fiery (burning) serpents among the people; and they bit the people, and many Israelites died. So the people came to Moses, and said, "We have sinned, for we have spoken against the LORD and against you; pray to the LORD, so that He will remove the serpents from us." So Moses prayed for the people. Then the LORD said to Moses, "Make a fiery serpent [of bronze] and set it on a pole; and everyone who is bitten will live when he looks at it." So Moses made a serpent of bronze and put it on the pole, and it happened that if a serpent had bitten any man, when he looked to the bronze serpent, he lived." -Numbers 21:6-9 AMP

Because of their constant complaints, the Lord sent poisonous snakes into the midst of the people and many that were bitten died. This punishment brought the people to a place of repentance, so coming to Moses they acknowledged their sin of speaking badly against the Lord and against Moses. The Israelites requested intercessory prayer from Moses on their behalf, so that the Lord would take away the serpents because death was all around them. Moses intercedes for the people and God instructs him to make a fiery serpent and to have it mounted on a pole, so that whoever had been bitten, if they would look upon the serpent, would live.

Intercessors people are bound to screw up over and over and over again, and will come requesting your prayers. Just pray because man didn't call you or choose you, God did.

Balaam Inquires of the Lord and Prophesies Blessings

Balaam had been hired by Balak to curse the children of Israel, but instead God put a blessing in his mouth for the people. Intercessors don't worry about who is hired to speak an ill word over your marriage, your children, your family or your finances. The Word of God says this concerning you, "You intended to harm me, but God intended it for good to accomplish what is now being done, the saving of many lives (Genesis 50:20 NIV)."

Their intent may have been to harm you, but God's got you. It will not work nor will it succeed. Intercessor God wants you to know, "Do not fret because of those who are evil or be envious of those who do wrong (Psalm 37:1 NIV)."

Don't fret intercessor just do what God has called you to do and watch him work it out for your good.

"And we know that all things work together for good to those who love God, to those who are called according to His purpose (Romans 8:28 NKJV)."

Joshua Succeeds Moses

"Then the LORD said to Moses, "Go up to this mountain (Nebo) [in the] Abarim [range] and look at the land I have given to the sons of Israel. When you have seen it, you too will be gathered to your people [in death], just as Aaron your brother was gathered; because in the Wilderness of Zin, during the strife of the congregation, you rebelled against My command to treat me as holy [by following My instruction] before their eyes at the water." (These are the waters of Meribah in Kadesh in the Wilderness of Zin.) "Then Moses spoke to the LORD, saying, " Let the LORD, the God of the spirits of all flesh, appoint a man over the congregation who will go out and come in before them, and will lead them out and bring them in, so that the congregation of the LORD will not be as sheep without a shepherd." The LORD said to Moses, "Take Joshua the son of Nun, a man in whom is the Spirit, and lay your hand on him; and have him stand before Eleazar the priest and before the whole congregation, and give him a commission in their sight. You shall put some of your authority and honor on him, so that all the congregation of the Israelites will obey him. He shall stand before Eleazar the priest, who shall inquire before the LORD for him by the judgment (decision) of the Urim. At Joshua's command the people shall go out and at his command they shall come in, he and all the congregation of Israel with him." Moses did as the LORD commanded him. He took Joshua and had him stand before Eleazar the priest and the whole congregation, and Moses laid his hands on Joshua and commissioned him, just as the LORD had commanded through Moses." -Numbers 27:12-23 AMP

Moses is commanded by God to go up to the mountain and have a look at the land that He has given to Israel. God says, "Moses when you have seen the land that I have promised my people then you will be gathered to your people in death just like your brother Aaron. Because you and Aaron disobeyed my command in the Wilderness of Zin and you did not honor me as holy before the eyes of the people this is as far as you will go.

Moses begins to intercede for the new leader as well as the people saying, "Before I transition I'm concerned for your people, that they will be like sheep with no shepherd, so the person that is your choice may he be a man of faith, courage, and humility. May he fear you, may he adhere to your laws and precepts, and may you give unto him a mantle for government. So the Lord says to Moses, "Take Joshua the son of Nun your assistant, a man that I know has the Spirit. I want you to have him stand before Eleazar the priest and before all the people and lay your hand on him and give him a commission in their sight. The laying of your hand on him will cause a transfer of some of your authority and honor onto him, so the congregation will obey him as they obeyed you. He is to stand before the priest who will inquire of the Lord on his behalf by the Urim and at his command the people shall go out and come in." Moses obeyed the Lord's instructions and did as he said.

Intercessors, may you intercede for and with your spiritual leader when it comes to restructuring the house of God or when a decision has to be made concerning who God has appointed to carry the torch. Moses interceded because he wanted the sheep covered by the right individual, just as you should. Pray until God speaks by way of vision, dream or audible voice. Your intercession is needed until he does.

Chapter Four

The Book of Deuteronomy

A Prayer of Blessing: *"May the LORD, the God of your fathers, add to you a thousand times as many as you are and bless you, just as He has promised you!"*
- Deuteronomy 1:11 AMP

A Prayer of Praise: *"Then I pleaded with the LORD at that time [for His favor], saying, 'O Lord GOD, You have only begun to show Your servant Your greatness and Your mighty hand; for what god is there in heaven or on earth that can do such works and mighty acts (miracles) as Yours? ~'I pray, let me go over and see the good land that is beyond the Jordan, that good hill country [with Hermon] and Lebanon.'"But the LORD was angry with me because of you [and your rebellion at Meribah], and would not listen to me; and the LORD said to me, 'Enough! Speak to Me no longer about this matter. ~'Go up to the top of [Mount] Pisgah and raise your eyes toward the west and north and south and east, and see it with your eyes, for you shall not cross this Jordan. ~'But command Joshua and encourage and strengthen him, for he shall go across and lead this people, and he will give them the land which you see as an inheritance.' So we stayed in the Valley opposite Beth-peor."*
-Deuteronomy 3:23-29AMP

No matter the outcome of a situation, always know that praying to God is the right thing to do. There may be times He may say, "Don't bring that matter to me again," but know this it's working for your good.

Intercessor, hear my heart concerning this matter. If you have been very consistent with presenting a matter to the Lord and he says to you, "Don't speak to me concerning this circumstance or situation ever again." Then do this, let it go.

"And we know that all things work together for good to those who love God, to those who are the called according to His purpose." -Romans 8:28 NKJV

A Prayer of Blessing: *"When you have eaten and are satisfied, then you shall bless the LORD your God for the good land which He has given you."* – Deuteronomy 8:10 AMP

It is important that you have a heart of gratitude for all that the Lord God gives to you. There is nothing wrong with praying a blessing of increase and favor over what sits before you. You are told to give thanks and having a grateful heart is a necessity.

"In everything give thanks; for this is the will of God in Christ Jesus for you." -1 Thessalonians 5:18 NKJV

A Prayer of Intercession for Aaron: *"The LORD was very angry with Aaron, angry [enough] to destroy him, so I also prayed for Aaron at the same time. I took your sinful thing, the calf which you had made, and burned it in the fire and thoroughly crushed it, grinding the metal thoroughly until it was as fine as dust; and I threw its dust into the brook that came down from the mountain."*
– Deuteronomy 9:20-21 AMP

"Be unceasing in prayer [praying perseveringly]; Thank [God] in everything [no matter what the circumstances may be, be thankful and give thanks], for this is the will of God for you

[who are] in Christ Jesus [the Revealer and Mediator of that will]." - 1 Thessalonians 5:17-18 AMPC

It may seem that God just doesn't get where you are coming from or that God doesn't understand your heart concerning a certain situation, but yes He does and His saying no to you is working for your good.

A Prayer of Agreement (Corporate Prayer)

The prayer of agreement or corporate prayer is when two or more people come together and agree with one another and with the Word of God that something specific will be done.

"All the elders of that city nearest to the dead man shall wash their hands over the heifer whose neck was broken in the valley; and they shall respond, and say, 'Our hands did not shed this blood, nor did our eyes see it. ~'Forgive Your people Israel whom You have redeemed, O LORD, and do not put the guilt of innocent blood among Your people Israel.' And the guilt of blood shall be forgiven them. So shall you remove the guilt of innocent blood from among you, when you do what is right in the sight of the LORD." - Deuteronomy 21:6-9 AMP

When you are gathered together in prayer and intercession with a group of fellow believers, you must possess a spirit of unity so that God's perfect and divine will can be prayed effectively. You must be in agreement that your agenda takes a back seat to the plan and purpose of God. Your thoughts should be not my will God but your will be done.

> *"Can two walk together, unless they are agreed?"*
> *-Amos 3:3 NKJV*

> *"These all continued with one accord in prayer and supplication, with the women and Mary the mother of Jesus, and with His brothers." -Acts 1:14 NKJV*

Prayer of Thanksgiving: *"And He has brought us to this place and has given us this land, a land flowing with milk and honey. ~'And now, look, I have brought the first of the produce of the ground which You, O LORD, have given me.' And you shall place it before the LORD your God, and shall worship before the LORD your God; and you and the Levite and the stranger (resident alien, foreigner) among you shall rejoice in all the good which the LORD your God has given you and your household. "When you have finished paying all the tithe of your produce the third year, [which is] the year of tithing, then you shall give it to the Levite, to the stranger, to the orphan, and to the widow, so that they may eat within the gates of your cities and be satisfied. You shall say before the LORD your God, 'I have removed the sacred portion (the tithe) from my house and also have given it to the Levite, to the stranger, to the orphan, and to the widow, in accordance with all that You have commanded me. I have not transgressed or forgotten any of Your commandments. ~'I have not eaten from the tithe while mourning, nor have I removed any of it when I was [ceremonially] unclean [making the tithe ceremonially unclean], nor offered any of it to the dead. I have listened to the voice of the LORD my God; I have done everything in accordance with all that You have commanded me. ~'Look down from Your holy dwelling above, from heaven, and bless Your people Israel, and the land which You have given us, as You have sworn to our fathers, a land [of plenty] flowing with milk and honey.'" -Deuteronomy 26:9-16 AMP*

Once the Lord brought the Israelites into the Promised Land, they were extremely thankful. There is absolutely nothing wrong with being thankful for all that God has done and will do. As 1 Thessalonians 5:18 NKJV says, " In everything give thanks; for this is the will of God in Christ Jesus for you."

A Prayer of Blessings Over the Twelve Tribes of Israel

Read Deuteronomy 33:1-29. In this passage of scripture, we see Moses pronouncing blessings over the tribe of Israel before his death. Please look closely at this scripture because it is the perfect example of prophetic intercession. Moses spoke so divinely concerning each tribe beginning with the Tribe of Reuben and ending with the Tribe of Asher.

Moses was the epitome of a leader of high regard. He was a leader who was in the process of transitioning, but before this happened he released over the Israelites a prophetic prayer of blessing. The children of Israel had come very far in their journeys through the wilderness and were open to hearing and to receiving the blessing pronounced over their individual tribe. I'm so grateful to God for spiritual leaders who know their assignment in the earth and have the know how to follow through and speak prophetically concerning our next. Prayers of blessings are important to the growth of every believer. The prayers of blessing offered up on behalf of others can transcend time and attach themselves to our future.

Chapter Five

The Book of Joshua

Whose Side Are You On?

"Now when Joshua was by Jericho, he looked up, and behold, a man was standing opposite him with his drawn sword in his hand, and Joshua went to him and said to him, "Are you for us or for our adversaries?" He said, "No; rather I have come now as captain of the army of the Lord." Then Joshua fell with his face toward the earth and bowed down, and said to him, "What does my lord have to say to his servant?" The captain of the Lord's army said to Joshua, "Remove your sandals from your feet, because the place where you are standing is holy (set apart to the Lord)." And Joshua did so. - Joshua 5:13-15 AMP

Joshua's position of humility in his response to the man is a reflection of his character. He didn't mind submitting himself to authority. God may ask you to do something that takes you out of your comfort zone. It's okay. Just follow through with what he says no matter how strange it may seem. What do you think would have happened to the city of Jericho if Joshua and the men of ward had walked around it only five times and then blew their rams horns and shouted? My guess is that the wall would not have come down.

"'But the sons of Israel acted unfaithfully and violated their obligation in regard to the things [off limits] under the ban [those things belonging to the LORD], for Achan, the son of Carmi, the son of Zabdi, the son of Zerah, from the tribe of Judah, took some of the things under the ban [for personal gain]. Therefore the anger of the LORD burned against the Israelites. Now Joshua sent men from Jericho to Ai, which is near Beth-aven, east of Bethel, and said to them, "Go up and spy out the land." So the men went up and spied out Ai. Then they returned to Joshua and said to him, "Do not make all the people go up [to fight]; have only about two thousand or three thousand men go up and attack Ai; do not make the entire army go up there, for they [of Ai] are few." So about three thousand men from the sons of Israel went up there, but they fled [in retreat] from the men of Ai. The men of Ai killed about thirty-six of Israel's men, and chased them from the gate as far as [the bluffs of] Shebarim and struck them down as they descended [the steep pass], so the hearts of the people melted [in despair and began to doubt God's promise] and became like water (disheartened). Then Joshua tore his clothes and fell face downward on the ground before the ark of the LORD until evening, he and the elders of Israel; and [with great sorrow] they put dust on their heads. Joshua said, "Alas, O Lord GOD, why have You brought this people across the Jordan at all, only to hand us over to the Amorites, to destroy us? If only we had been willing to live beyond the Jordan! O Lord, what can I say now that [the army of] Israel has turned back [in retreat and fled] before their enemies? For the Canaanites and all the inhabitants of the land will hear about it, and will surround us and cut off our name from the earth. And what will You do for Your great name [to keep it from dishonor]?" So the LORD said to Joshua, "Get up! Why is it that you have fallen on your face? Israel has sinned; they have also transgressed My covenant which I commanded them [to keep]. They have even taken some of the things under the ban, and they have both stolen and denied [the theft]. Moreover, they have also put the stolen objects among their own things. That is why the soldiers of Israel could not stand [and defend themselves] before their enemies; they turned their backs [and ran] before them, because they have become accursed. I will not be with you anymore unless you destroy the things under the ban from among you. Rise up! Consecrate the people and say, 'Consecrate yourselves for tomorrow, for thus says the LORD, the

God of Israel: "There are things under the ban among you, O Israel. You cannot stand [victorious] before your enemies until you remove the things under the ban from among you." ~'In the morning you shall come forward by your tribes. And it shall be that the tribe which the LORD chooses by lot shall come forward by families, and the family which the LORD chooses shall come forward by [separate] households, and the household which the LORD chooses shall come forward man by man. ~'It shall be that the one who is chosen with the things under the ban shall be [killed and his body] burned with fire, he and all that belongs to him, because he has transgressed the covenant of the LORD, and because he has done a disgraceful and disobedient thing in Israel.'"

-Joshua 7:1-15 AMP

Intercessors, there may come a time when you know you have done all that God has told you to do and through all of that, you still lose a battle. Like Joshua you may feel like God has let you down and not kept His word to you. But hear me good. In moments like this you must examine your camp. Make sure no one attached to you has taken the accursed thing. Make sure no one has stolen from God what is rightfully His. Achan stole from God and caused thirty-six men to lose their lives at Ai. This should have been a battle they won, but it resulted in loss for them because of the sin in their midst. If things are beginning to go wrong for you, intercede until the Holy Spirit speaks to you and directs you to those hidden areas of sin that need to be exposed and repented for. I guarantee if it is there, it will be uncovered and revealed in time. Achan's lies caused not only his death, but the death of everything attached to him as well. Intercessors, be careful, be watchful and intercede.

"Behold, You desire truth in the inward parts, And in the hidden part You will make me to know wisdom."

- Psalm 51:6 NKJV

The Sun and Moon Stand Still

"Then Joshua spoke to the LORD on the day when the LORD handed over the Amorites to the sons of Israel, and Joshua said in the sight of Israel, "Sun, stand still at Gibeon, And moon, in the Valley of Aijalon." So the sun stood still, and the moon stopped, Until the nation [of Israel] took vengeance upon their enemies. Is it not written in the Book of Jashar? So the sun stood still in the middle of the sky and was in no hurry to go down for about a whole day. There has not been a day like that before it or after it, when the LORD listened to (heeded) the voice of a man; for the LORD was fighting for Israel. Then Joshua and all Israel with him returned to the camp at Gilgal."
- Joshua 10:12-15 AMP

Intercessors as we take a look at Joshua, Moses' predecessor, Joshua was a man of intercession as well.
He was there with Moses until Moses transitioned and went to glory; and He was there every time the people did wrong. He had a bird's eye view of intercession at it's finest. He saw what kept Moses from crossing over to the Promised Land and probably said to himself, "I'm not going out like that. I want all that God has in store for me."

You must have faith in your Christian walk. It took faith for Joshua to ask that the sun and the moon stand completely still in the sky, and it was that same faith that caused it to happen. Joshua interceded and the Lord answered his prayer.

Chapter Six

The Book of Judges

Who Will Lead Us Now?

"Now it came about after the death of Joshua, that the sons (descendants) of Israel (Jacob) asked the LORD, "Who shall go up first for us against the Canaanites, to fight against them?" And the LORD said, "Judah shall go up [first]; behold, I have given the land into his hand." And [the tribe of the sons of] Judah said to [the tribe of the sons of] Simeon his brother, "Come up with me into my allotted territory, so that we may fight against the Canaanites; and I likewise will go with you into your allotted territory." So Simeon went with him. Then Judah went up, and the LORD gave the Canaanites and the Perizzites into their hand, and they struck down in defeat ten thousand men at Bezek. Then they found Adoni-bezek in Bezek and fought against him, and they struck down in defeat the Canaanites and the Perizzites. But Adoni-bezek fled; and they pursued him and caught him and cut off his thumbs and his big toes. Adoni-bezek said, "Seventy kings with their thumbs and big toes cut off used to gather up scraps of food under my table; as I have done [to others], so God has repaid me." So they brought him to Jerusalem, and he died there." - Judges 1:1-7 AMP

In this passage of scripture, Joshua has passed away and there is still more land to be distributed among the tribes so the children of Israel offered up prayer of petition concerning who would take the lead in the battle and God said that Judah would go first because I have given the land into his hand and the tribes of Judah came into agreement that Simeon would help Judah fight and get their land and after it had been conquered, they would help Simeon to take their land.

"Now this is the confidence that we have in Him, that if we ask anything according to His will, He hears us. And if we know that He hears us, whatever we ask, we know that we have the petitions that we have asked of Him." - I John 5:14-15 NKJV

As intercessors you have the right to make your requests known to God. Like Judah, submit your request to God and ask according to His will. It doesn't matter how small you may feel the matter is, ask according to God's will and He will not only hear you, but He will also answer.
    Your request might be Lord Jesus send someone my way that knows how to write a grant proposal or I need a new prayer partner, someone that has a heart for prayer like I do, or I need a new loan to get my business started should I wait now or wait until a more favorable time." Whatever it is just ask Him. You may even wonder whether or not something is God's will in that moment and inquire as to what you should do. Here's your answer...

" Then you will call upon Me and go and pray to Me, and I will listen to you. And you will seek Me and find Me, when you search for Me with all your heart."
                                        – Jeremiah 29:12-13 NKJV

Prayers of Lamentation

"Then the Israelites did evil in the sight of the LORD; and the LORD gave them into the hand of Midian for seven years. The [powerful] hand of Midian prevailed against Israel. Because of

Midian the sons of Israel made for themselves the dens (hideouts), which were in the mountains, and the caves and the [mountain] strongholds. For it was whenever Israel had sown [their seed] that the Midianites would come up with the Amalekites and the people of the east and go up against them. So they would camp against them and destroy the crops of the land as far as Gaza, and leave no sustenance in Israel as well as no sheep, ox, or donkey. For they would come up with their livestock and their tents, and they would come in as numerous as locusts; both they and their camels were innumerable. So they came into the land to devastate it. So Israel was greatly impoverished because of the Midianites, and the Israelites cried out to the LORD [for help]. Now it came about when they cried out to the LORD because of Midian, that the LORD sent a prophet to the Israelites, and he said to them, "Thus says the LORD, the God of Israel, 'I brought you up from Egypt and brought you out of the house of slavery. ~'And I rescued you from the hand of the Egyptians and from the hand of all who oppressed you, and drove them out before you and gave you their land, and I said to you, "I am the LORD your God; you shall not fear the gods of the Amorites in whose land you live." But you have not listened to and obeyed My voice.""

-Judges 6:1-10 AMP

As you look at the book of Judges, you will notice a pattern of willful sinning and open rebellion with the children of Israel. In the second chapter of Judges, God sends the angel of the Lord to confront them concerning their willful disobedience towards him and says that he has always been faithful to them but they have not been faithful to him, and for this cause he would not drive their enemies from before them. They were going to have to live with their enemies having the upper hand and mistreating them, and there would be nothing they could do but lift their voices and lament.

Intercessors, just like the children of Israel, God has instructed us on the dos and don'ts in our lives; and He chastens those He loves. Maybe in your own life you have tried to persuade God to change his mind concerning what you willingly walked into, that thing that you just had to have that was not good for you. And because we have free will God allowed you to run after that thing that you desired the most and now you have to deal with the consequences of your actions just like the children of Israel. As you can see in the scripture, God raised up multiple deliverers and a few are named-Othinel, the younger brother of Caleb, Ehud the son of Gera, Shamgar the son of Anath, Deborah a prophetess and the wife of Lappidoth, Barak the son of Abinoam, and Gideon the son of Joash the Abbiezrite.

Judges the sixth chapter talks about another prophet whose name is unknown, but still God uses him to help the people remember their transgressions toward Him. After hearing the prayers of lamentation by His people, every person named above was handpicked by God to deliver the children of Israel from the hand of their oppressors. Let me ask you a few questions. How many deliverers has God raised up for you? How many prophets were sent your way that you didn't even know the name of, but God still spoke through them? How many people has God allowed to align with you until you were set free? How many people labored with you until you came forth? How many people has God used to fight battles for you in the spirit realm until that thing was broken off of your life?

Dr. Anthony Earl put it this way, "Pay attention to details." How many billboards have you passed on the interstate that said, "Let go and let God"? God speaks in various ways. We just need to listen a little more intently. Intercessors, distress, suffering and pain are a part of every believer's life, but let's make sure that when we cry out to God in lamentation it's not attached to sin and willful disobedience. God will answer but in His timing.

Gideon Is Visited

"Now the Angel of the LORD came and sat under the terebinth tree at Ophrah, which belonged to Joash the Abiezrite, and his son Gideon was beating wheat in the wine press [instead of the threshing floor] to [hide it and] save it from the Midianites. And the Angel of the LORD appeared to him and said to him, "The LORD is with you, O brave man." But Gideon said to him, "Please my lord, if the LORD is with us, then why has all this happened to us? And where are all His wondrous works which our fathers told us about when they said, 'Did not the LORD bring us up from Egypt?' But now the LORD has abandoned us and put us into the hand of Midian." The LORD turned to him and said, "Go in this strength of yours and save Israel from the hand of Midian. Have I not sent you?" But Gideon said to Him, "Please Lord, how am I to rescue Israel? Behold, my family is the least [significant] in Manasseh, and I am the youngest (smallest) in my father's house." The LORD answered him, "I will certainly be with you, and you will strike down the Midianites as [if they were only] one man." Gideon replied to Him, "If I have found any favor in Your sight, then show me a sign that it is You who speaks with me. Please do not depart from here until I come back to You, and bring my offering and place it before You." And He said, "I will wait until you return."" -Judges 6:11-18

Just like Gideon, assignments will come from the Lord and you, like Gideon, may feel like you are inadequate or that you were born or raised in a family that didn't have much substance so how can God even think to use little old you. But an assignment from God is just that, an assignment. Oftentimes you may go into supplication or intercession, praying out of your own will and not God's. I promise you there is no excuse that has been uttered that God has not heard, so like Gideon you are in prayer and you are asking for a sign to prove that what you dreamed or what you saw in an open eye vision or what was prophesied to you was really from the Lord. It's okay, you sound a lot like one of God's most beloved disciples, Peter.

"Peter replied to Him, "Lord, if it is [really] You, command me to come to You on the water." He said, "Come!" So Peter got out of the boat, and walked on the water and came toward Jesus.""
-Matthew 14:28-29 AMP

When you are in supplication or intercession concerning a matter and a little reassurance is needed, God will provide answers so that you walk into your assignment with greater confidence and trust in Him. Gideon was like a babe when it came to what God wanted to do through him. Just like Gideon, we have babes in Christ who are new to how God works. Like He does for all of His children, God will confirm what may have been uttered concerning which way to go, what to do and how to do it. God will not leave you without an answer. So if he says stand still and do nothing, well do just that. But let me say this as well, as we grow in faith, learn how to press through this life of holiness, and study the Word of God on a daily basis, confirmation will begin to come quite often through scripture.

" I will instruct you and teach you in the way you should go; I will guide you with My eye." – Psalms 32:8 NKJV

The Present of Gideon Is Now A Sacrifice

"Then Gideon went and prepared a young goat and unleavened bread from an ephah of flour. The meat he put in a basket and the broth in a pot, and he brought the food to Him under the oak (terebinth) and presented it. The Angel of God said to him, "Take the meat and unleavened bread and lay them on this rock, and pour out the broth [over them]." And he did so. Then the Angel of the Lord put out the end of the staff that was in His hand and touched the meat and the unleavened bread; and fire flared up from the rock and consumed the meat and the unleavened bread. Then the Angel of the Lord vanished from his sight. When Gideon realized [without any doubt] that He was the Angel of the Lord, he declared, "Oh no, Lord God! For now I have seen the Angel of the Lord face to face [and I am doomed]!" The Lord said to him, "Peace to you, do not be afraid; you shall not die." Then Gideon built an altar there to the Lord and named it The Lord is Peace. To this day it is still in Ophrah, of the Abiezrites." -Judges 6:19-24

While the Angel of the Lord waits under the terebinth tree, Gideon is busy preparing his guests a meal. As he approaches, the angel tells him to place everything that he has so carefully prepared on the rock and to pour the broth over them. Gideon does as he is instructed. Look at how Gideon follows instructions. He never says, " Excuse me, I've prepared this wonderful meal and you want me to take it and place it on a rock." He simply did as he was told. As intercessors, we must learn to listen and follow God's instructions.

After following the angel's instructions, Gideon eventually realizes that he has had a divine encounter, but not until the angel has already vanished. Gideon begins to panic and fears that this encounter means that he is going to die. God speaks peace to him and assures him that he is not going to die, so Gideon builds an altar to God and names it "The Lord Is Peace."

Intercessor, there is much work for you to do. God is not finished with you yet, just watch and see.

Gideon Receives A Detailed Assignment

"Now on that same night the LORD said to Gideon, "Take your father's bull, the second bull seven years old, and tear down the altar of Baal that belongs to your father, and cut down the Asherah that is beside it; and build an altar to the LORD your God on top of this mountain stronghold [with stones laid down] in an orderly way. Then take the second bull and offer a burnt sacrifice using the wood of the Asherah which you shall cut down." Then Gideon took ten men of his servants and did just as the LORD had told him; but because he was too afraid of his father's household (relatives) and the men of the city to do it during daylight,he did it at night. Early the next morning when the men of the city got up, they discovered that the altar of Baal was torn down, and the Asherah which was beside it was cut down, and the second bull was offered on the altar which had been built. So they said to one another, "Who has done this thing?" When they searched about and inquired, they were told, "Gideon the son of Joash did it." Then the men of the city said to Joash, "Bring out your son, so that he may be executed, because he has torn down the altar of Baal and cut down the Asherah which was beside it." But Joash said to all who stood against him, "Will you plead for Baal? Will you save him? Whoever pleads for Baal shall be put to death while it is still morning. If Baal is a god, let him defend himself, because someone has torn down his altar." Therefore on that day he named Gideon Jerubbaal, meaning, "Let Baal plead," because he had torn down his altar. Then all the Midianites and the Amalekites and the people of the east assembled together; and

they crossed over [the Jordan] and camped in the Valley of Jezreel. So the Spirit of the LORD clothed Gideon [and empowered him]; and he blew a trumpet, and the Abiezrites were called together [as a militia] to follow him. He sent messengers throughout [the tribe of] Manasseh, and the fighting men were also called together to follow him; and he sent messengers to [the tribes of] Asher, Zebulun, and Naphtali, and they came up to meet them."* -Judges 6:25-35 AMP

God is so detail orientated. When we allow Him to lead us, He will give us step-by-step instructions. All we have to do is listen and obey. When we do it God's way, He will also assist us and send us the help we need to carry out the assignment.

"I will instruct you and teach you in the way you should go; I will guide you with My eye." -Psalms 32:8 NKJV

The Fleece and Gideon's Prayers of Supplication

"Then Gideon said to God, "If You are going to rescue Israel through me, as You have spoken, behold, I will put a fleece of [freshly sheared] wool on the threshing floor. If there is dew only on the fleece, and it is dry on all the ground [around it], then I will know that You will rescue Israel through me, as You have said." And it was so. When he got up early the next morning and squeezed the dew out of the fleece, he wrung from it a bowl full of water. Then Gideon said to God, "Do not let your anger burn against me, so that I may speak once more. Please let me make a test once more with the fleece; now let only the fleece be dry, and let there be dew on all the ground." God did so that night; for it was dry only on the fleece, and there was dew on all the ground [around it]."

-Judges 6:36-40 AMP

When you are in supplication or intercession concerning a matter and a little reassurance is needed, God will provide answers so that you can walk into the assignment with greater confidence and so that your trust level can be built up. Gideon was like a babe when it came to what God wanted to do through him, so there are babes in Christ who are new to how God works; and so God will confirm what may have been uttered concerning which way to go, what to do, and how to do it. God will not leave you without an answer, so if He says stand still and do nothing, well just do that. Stand and do nothing. As you grow in faith and learn how to press through this life of holiness, and as you walk with Him in the word, daily confirmation from the scriptures will come quite often.

Gideon Seeks Confirmation

As the book of Judges progresses, we once again see Gideon needing confirmation on whether or not God is going to rescue Israel through him, as He had already told him He would do.

As intercessors, we must deal with doubt and unbelief because they are the primary drivers behind constantly asking God to prove Himself. This may happen when you are a babe in Christ, but by no means should it be the norm for a person that has been saved for quite some time. If you are a seasoned saint who finds yourself needing confirmation from God, deal with your doubt and unbelief.

"But without faith it is impossible to please Him, for he who comes to God must believe that He is, and that He is a rewarder of those who diligently seek Him." - Hebrews 11:6 NKJV

The Prayers of Lamentation

"After Abimelech died, Tola the son of Puah, the son of Dodo, a man of Issachar, arose to save Israel; and he lived in Shamir, in the hill country of Ephraim. Tola judged Israel for twenty-three years; then he died and was buried in Shamir. After him, Jair the Gileadite arose, and he judged Israel for twenty-two years. He had thirty sons who rode on thirty donkeys, and they had thirty towns in the land of Gilead that are called Havvoth-jair (towns of Jair) to this day. And Jair died and was buried in Kamon. Then the Israelites again did what was evil in the sight of the LORD; they served the Baals, the Ashtaroth (female deities), the gods of Aram (Syria), the gods of Sidon, the gods of Moab, the gods of the Ammonites, and the gods of the Philistines. They abandoned the LORD and did not serve Him. So the anger of the LORD was kindled against Israel, and He sold them into the hands of the Philistines and the Ammonites, and they oppressed and crushed Israel that year. For eighteen years they oppressed all the Israelites who were beyond the Jordan in the land of the Amorites, which is in Gilead. The Ammonites crossed the Jordan to fight against Judah, Benjamin, and the house of Ephraim, so that Israel was greatly distressed. Then the Israelites cried out to the LORD [for help], saying, "We have sinned against You, because we have abandoned (rejected) our God and have served the Baals." The LORD said to the Israelites, " Did I not rescue you from the Egyptians, the Amorites, the Ammonites, and the Philistines? Also when the Sidonians, the Amalekites, and the Maonites oppressed and crushed you, you cried out to Me, and I rescued you from their hands. Yet you have abandoned (rejected) Me and served other gods; therefore I will no longer rescue you. Go, cry out to the gods you have chosen; let them rescue you in your time of distress." The Israelites said to the LORD, "We have sinned, do to us whatever seems good to You; only please rescue us this day." So they removed the foreign gods from *among them and served the LORD; and He could bear the misery of Israel no longer. Then the Ammonites were assembled together and they camped in Gilead. And the sons of Israel assembled and camped at Mizpah. The people, the leaders of Gilead (Israel) said to one another, "Who is the man who will begin to fight against the Ammonites? He shall become head over all the inhabitants of Gilead.""*

-Judges 10:1-18 AMP

When you are in the midst of a battle, and you have not only been praying for your circumstances and situation, but also others as well, and your adversary is stirred up and advancing your way, know this one thing. While you're trying to figure out who is on your side, God has already taken care of those details. In most instances, you are going to have to rely on the strength that God has given you. As my spiritual mother Prophetess Jacqueline Rhymes often reminds me, " Daughter, God has given you the strength of a wild oxen so plow and go deeper."

You should already be dressed for battle, so that when it hits your doorstep you are not surprised.

"Put on the full armor of God [for His precepts are like the splendid armor of a heavily-armed soldier], so that you may be able to [successfully] stand up against all the schemes and the strategies and the deceits of the devil." - Ephesians 6:11 AMP

A Vow That Must Be Paid

In Judges 11: 29-40, the power and the strength of the Lord come upon Jephthah and he passed over Gilead and Manasseh and from Mizpah of Gilead until he came to the Ammonites. Jephthah makes a vow to the Lord saying, " If you will give my enemy into my hand then whatever comes out of the doors of my house to meet me upon my return from the battle will become yours; and I will offer it to you as a burnt offering."

Intercessors let me interject and say that we cannot possibly condemn Jephthah for his vow, because most of us have also made a vow or two to the Lord. We've said things like Lord if you bless me with this new job I'll pay my tithes and offering. The Lord keeps His end of the bargain, but more often than not we don't keep ours. So before we judge Jephthah too harshly, we should closely examine ourselves.

Jephthah and his men cross over to where the Ammonites are and ultimately win the battle. In returning from battle, Jephtah's daughter is the first to greet him. Because of his vow, Jephthah now has to determine whether or not he will follow through with giving his daughter up as an offering. Ultimately, he doesn't. Instead he separates her from the company of men they lived among, and she lives unmarried for the rest of her life.

The lesson we can all take away from Jephthah is that it is better to not vow, than to vow and then break it. Be careful of the words you release from your mouth. They can prove to be harmful to those closest to you.

Israel Does Evil Again

Read Judges 13:1-25. In this passage of scripture, we once again see that the vicious cycle of idolatry has reared its head. The people have corrupted themselves once again, and as a result God delivers them into the hands of the Philistines for forty years. In the midst of this, God once again looks on their struggles and oppression and prepares a deliverer to execute His judgment on the

Philistines. This deliverer will come through the loins of the wife of Manoah, a woman who is unable to have children. The child that eventually comes forth is Samson, a Nazirite from birth.

Samson grows up to become a strong and courageous man. The Bible tells us that "The Spirit of the Lord moved upon him at time and he abstained from wine or any strong drink but he excelled in courage and strength."

In Death Samson Gets Revenge

"Then Samson called to the Lord and said, "O Lord God, please remember me and please strengthen me just this one time, O God, and let me take vengeance on the Philistines for my two eyes." [29] Samson took hold of the two middle [support] pillars on which the house rested, and braced himself against them, one with his right hand and the other with his left. And Samson said, "Let me die with the Philistines!" And he stretched out with all his might [collapsing the support pillars], and the house fell on the lords and on all the people who were in it. So the dead whom he killed at his death were more than those whom he had killed during his life. Then his brothers and his father's entire [tribal] household came down, took him, and brought him up; and they buried him in the tomb of Manoah his father, [which was] between Zorah and Eshtaol. So Samson had judged Israel for twenty years."

-Judges 16:28-31 AMP

Samson had been brought to a low place. By this time, he had experienced ridicule, heartbreak, treachery and deceit from someone he loved and trusted, and sold him out for 5,500 pieces of silver. Despite all of this, Samson was still God's choice to bring about the defeat of the

Philistines. Intercessors, like Samson you may have pursued after someone or something that betrayed you, but God is not a deceiver. He is compassionate towards us, even when we mess up. God is compassionate enough to hear us when we call, but don't make the mistake that Samson made. Instead of asking to die, turn the tables on your adversaries and make a bold declaration that you are not going to die, you are going to live because unlike Samson you are ready to make a comeback.

"I shall not die, but live, And declare the works of the LORD."
-Psalms 118:17 NKJV

Benjamin Is Defeated

The sons of Israel went up and wept before the LORD until evening, and asked of the LORD, "Shall we advance again to battle against the sons of our brother Benjamin?" And the LORD said, "Go up against them." So the sons of Israel came against the sons of Benjamin the second day. And [the fighting men from the tribe of] Benjamin went out of Gibeah against them the second day and again struck to the ground the sons of Israel, eighteen thousand men, all of whom were swordsmen. Then all the sons of Israel and all the people went up and came to Bethel and wept; and they sat there before the LORD and fasted that day until evening and offered burnt offerings and peace offerings before the LORD. And the sons of Israel inquired of the LORD (for the ark of the covenant of God was there [at Bethel] in those days, and Phinehas the son of Eleazar, the son of Aaron, ministered before it in those days), saying,

"Shall I yet again go out to battle against the sons of my brother Benjamin, or shall I quit?" And the LORD said, "Go up, for tomorrow I will hand them over to you."
– Judges 20:23-28 AMP

Intercessors may you never judge another man's sins. Instead do a heart evaluation on yourself. Examine why you feel the way you feel about a certain individual. Assess why you can't be around them and determine if it is them or if it's just you. Make sure that your motives are pure and not selfish. Repent and come clean before the Lord. Empty out so that God can fill you up again.

I promise there is nothing wrong with asking God to show you what's on the inside that has been lying dormant for some time. Dealing with it is necessary for your growth. Don't pretend like you're perfect. Deal with those imperfect parts of you that you don't like, so that you can pray effectively and be all that God has called you to be.

"The heart is deceitful above all things, And desperately wicked; Who can know it? –Jeremiah 17:9 NKJV

Lamentations Offered for the Tribe of Benjamin

"Now the men of Israel had sworn [an oath] at Mizpah, "None of us shall give his daughter in marriage to [a man of] Benjamin." So the people came to Bethel and sat there before God until evening, and lifted up their voices and wept bitterly. They said, "O LORD, God of Israel, why has this come about in Israel, that there should be today one tribe missing from Israel?" And the next day the people got up early and built an altar there and offered burnt offerings and peace offerings."
– Judges 21:1-4 AMP

When you have labored diligently in intercession with much weeping and anguish of heart because death has taken someone close, don't stay in that place of sorrow. Instead, rise up and give God glory, honor and praise for enabling you to be strength to someone who needed it, but didn't know it.

"You will seek me and find me when you search for me with all your heart." -Jeremiah 29:13 CSB

Chapter Seven

The Book of Ruth

Prayers of Blessings

"But Naomi said to her two daughters-in-law, "Go back, each of you return to your mother's house. May the LORD show kindness to you as you have shown kindness to the dead and to me. May the LORD grant that you find rest, each one in the home of her husband." Then she kissed them [goodbye], and they wept aloud." - Ruth 1:8-9 AMP

In this passage of scripture Naomi's husband, Elimelech, and her two sons Mahlon and Chillion have died, leaving her with her two daughters-in-law, Orpah and Ruth. Both Orpah and Ruth are Moabite women. Naomi tells them to return back to their former homes. Inspite of her losses, Naomi finds strength and fortitude and prays not for herself, but for her daughters-in-law, that the Lord would bless them. The Lord answers her prayers.

"It was then that Boaz came back from Bethlehem and said to the reapers, "The LORD be with you!" And they answered him, "The LORD bless you!"" – Ruth 2:4 AMP

The prayers of blessings are such powerful prayers to pray on a daily basis. We have the power in our mouths to pronounce a blessing, so why not do it? Boaz pronounced blessings on those that were part of his workforce. For those of you reading this that are entrepreneurs, why not try doing this? Bless those that are helping you to push your business to the next level.

Speak a blessing over those that are always looking out for others. Learn to speak increase upon their finances. Speak a blessing over young men or women who are remaining chaste before the Lord. Bless them and pray that they hold on to God until the right mate comes along. You may know of a family where the woman may not be able to conceive, bless them. You have the authority to speak to her womb and command increase to come. Tell it to line up with what the word declares, that she is fruitful and her womb will multiply. Tell her womb, " Behold, children are a heritage and gift from the LORD, the fruit of the womb a reward (Psalm 127:3 AMP)."

Women of God, let's learn how to speak a blessing over other women. Let go of competition because it's not from God. Open up your mouth and bless your sister because she needs it.

Chapter Eight

The Book of 1 Samuel

Hannah's Travail

So Hannah arose after they had finished eating and drinking in Shiloh. Now Eli the priest was sitting on the seat by the doorpost of the tabernacle of the LORD. And she was in bitterness of soul, and prayed to the LORD and wept in anguish. Then she made a vow and said, "O LORD of hosts, if You will indeed look on the affliction of Your maidservant and remember me, and not forget Your maidservant, but will give Your maidservant a male child, then I will give him to the LORD all the days of his life, and no razor shall come upon his head." And it happened, as she continued praying before the LORD, that Eli watched her mouth. Now Hannah spoke in her heart; only her lips moved, but her voice was not heard. Therefore Eli thought she was drunk. So Eli said to her, "How long will you be drunk? Put your wine away from you!" But Hannah answered and said, "No, my lord, I am a woman of sorrowful spirit. I have drunk neither wine nor intoxicating drink, but have poured out my soul before the LORD." Do not consider your maidservant a wicked woman, for out of the abundance of my complaint and grief I have spoken until now." Then Eli answered and said, t "Go in peace, and the God of Israel grant your petition which you have asked of Him." And she said, "Let your maidservant find favor in your sight." So the woman went her way and ate, and her face was no longer sad. Then they rose early in the morning and worshiped before the LORD, and returned and came to their house at Ramah. And Elkanah knew Hannah his wife, and the LORD remembered her. So it came to pass in the process of time that Hannah conceived and bore a son, and called his name Samuel, saying, "Because I have asked for him from the LORD."

- 1 Samuel 1:9-20 AMP

Just as Hannah was faced with a womb that did not give birth to what her heart desired, you too may be dealing with a similar situation. I'm sure that just like Hannah you have prayed and prayed and seemingly nothing has happened or changed. But this next time will be different. Change your tactics and shift the way that you pray the situation through. Perhaps like Hannah you've decided that enough is enough and I must go deeper because I need what I'm facing to touch the heart of God. I need God to take notice of what I'm going through. I need God to move on my behalf. I feel you intercessors. For both you and Hannah it is the travailing before God that does it. Through your travail God will speak a word, a clear prophetic word that He will honor and bring to pass.

After God delivered on his promise to Hannah, Hannah prays prophetically concerning his power, dignity and authority. She blesses the Lord and acknowledges that there is no one holy like Him. Like Hannah, prophesy about the goodness of the Lord. Make bold declarations over your life when God keeps His word, as He always does. Pour love, honor and respect onto him. Let your adversaries know that your God always comes through no matter what. Let them know how faithful your God has been to you. Open your mouth wide and tell it like Hannah. Release a sound of praise, thanksgiving and worship unto the Lord.

Know that when you pray prophetic prayers like Hannah, it shifts your trust in God to another level. Your faith will begin to grow by leaps and bounds, and you obtain a greater authority to do what is required of you.

Praying prophetically is praying the heart of God, the will of God and the mind of God.

Eli's Prayer of Blessing

"Now Samuel was ministering before the LORD, as a child dressed in a linen ephod [a sacred item of priestly clothing]. Moreover, his mother would make him a little robe and would bring it up to him each year when she came up with her husband to offer the yearly sacrifice. Then Eli would bless Elkanah and his wife and say, "May the LORD give you children by this woman in place of the one she asked for which was dedicated to the LORD." Then they would return to their own home. And [the time came when] the LORD visited Hannah, so that she conceived and gave birth to three sons and two daughters. And the boy Samuel grew before the LORD."
-1 Samuel 2:18-21 AMP

Samuel Learns the Voice of God and How to Respond

Read 1 Samuel 3:1-21. In this passage of scripture we see the Lord making Himself known to the child, Samuel, but to the priest Eli he said nothing. If we are not careful, and neglect to straighten out our sinful matters, we could end up just like Eli. Intercessors our hearts and our motives must be pure before God. Samuel was a very young child but God still spoke to him even after he had stopped speaking to Eli the priest. God speaks to the pure in heart, those who desire a more intimate relationship with Him. The child Samuel couldn't make a distinction about who it was that was calling his name, but he did hear his name being called. How many times has God called you by name? It may not have been audible, but in your spirit you knew it was Him trying to connect with you and let you in on a few well-hidden secrets.

Intercessors guard your hearts. God is calling your name don't miss out on what he is saying.

Samuel Prays for the People

"Then Samuel said to all the house of Israel, "If you are returning to the LORD with all your heart, remove the foreign gods and the Ashtaroth (pagan goddesses) from among you and direct your hearts to the LORD and serve Him only; and He will rescue you from the hand of the Philistines." So the Israelites removed the Baals and the Ashtaroth and served the LORD alone. Samuel said, "Gather all Israel together at Mizpah and I will pray to the LORD for you." So they gathered at Mizpah, and drew water and poured it out before the LORD, and fasted on that day and said there, "We have sinned against the LORD." And Samuel judged the Israelites at Mizpah. Now when the Philistines heard that the Israelites had gathered at Mizpah, the lords (governors) of the Philistines went up against Israel. And when the Israelites heard it, they were afraid of the Philistines. And the sons of Israel said to Samuel, "Do not cease to cry out to the LORD our God for us, so that He may save us from the hand of the Philistines." So Samuel took a nursing lamb and offered it as a whole burnt offering to the LORD; and Samuel cried out to the LORD for Israel and the LORD answered him. As Samuel was offering up the burnt offering, the Philistines approached for the battle against Israel. Then the LORD thundered with a great voice that day against the Philistines and threw them into confusion, and they were defeated and fled before Israel. And the men of Israel came out of Mizpah and pursued the Philistines, and struck them down as far as [the territory] below Beth-car. Then Samuel took a stone and set it between Mizpah and Shen, and he named it Ebenezer (stone of help), saying, "Thus far the LORD has helped us.""– 1 Samuel 7:3-12 AMP

The children of Israel have turned away from God and Samuel instructs them to get rid of every idol god they served in order to be effective in what God had called them to do,

Intercessors put away every false god and all those things that displease Him. Empty yourself before Him so that when you are praying for others, your prayers will not be hindered. Remove every blockage out of your way. Whatever or whoever it is it should not receive more glory than God.

Israel Rejects God and Samuel Prays

"And it came about when Samuel was old that he appointed his sons as judges over Israel. Now the name of his firstborn was Joel, and the name of his second, Abijah; they were judging in Beersheba. His sons, however, did not walk in his ways, but turned aside after dishonest gain, took bribes, and perverted justice. Then all the elders of Israel gathered together and came to Samuel at Ramah and said to him, "Look, you have grown old, and your sons do not walk in your ways. Now appoint us a king to judge us [and rule over us] like all the other nations." But their demand displeased Samuel when they said, "Give us a king to judge and rule over us." So Samuel prayed to the LORD. The LORD said to Samuel, "Listen to the voice of the people in regard to all that they say to you, for they have not rejected you, but they have rejected Me from being King over them. Like all the deeds which they have done since the day that I brought them up from Egypt even to this day--in that they have abandoned (rejected) Me and served other gods--so they are doing to you also. So now listen to their voice; only solemnly warn them and tell them the ways of the king who will reign over them."" – 1 Samuel 8:1-9 AMP

Intercessors allow me to help you here. If you feel you have become too old to carry out the work of the Lord, inquire of God on who your successor should be. Just because your blood child may be in ministry with you, doesn't mean they are the one that God has chosen to cover His sheep. Intercede until God speaks and says this is who I have called and chosen for the work. Don't move until the answer is a sure one, you don't want to put a wolf over the sheep. Just wait, God will reveal who it should be.

"As the Father knows Me, even so I know the Father; and I lay down My life for the sheep." - John 10:15 NKJV

Samuel Continues to Pray

"So now, take your stand and see this great thing which the LORD will do before your eyes. Is it not [the beginning of the] wheat harvest today? I will call to the LORD and He will send thunder and rain; then you will know [without any doubt], and see that your evil which you have done is great in the sight of the LORD by asking for yourselves a king." So Samuel called to the LORD [in prayer], and He sent thunder and rain that day; and all the people greatly feared the LORD and Samuel. Then all the people said to Samuel, "Pray to the LORD your God for your servants, so that we will not die, for we have added to all our sins this evil--to ask for a king for ourselves." Samuel said to the people, "Do not be afraid. You have [indeed] done all this evil; yet do not turn away from following the LORD, but serve the LORD with all your heart. You must not turn away, for then you would go after futile things which cannot profit or rescue, because they are futile. The LORD will not abandon His people for His great name's sake, because the LORD has been pleased to make you a people for

Himself."Moreover, as for me, far be it from me that I should sin against the LORD by ceasing to pray for you; but I will instruct you in the good and right way. "*Only fear the LORD [with awe and profound reverence] and serve Him faithfully with all your heart; for consider what great things He has done for you. But if you still do evil, both you and your king will be swept away [to destruction].*"" – 1 Samuel 12:16-25 AMP

Intercessors pray, pray, and pray some more. Even as Samuel interceded for the people's desire to be like the surrounding nations, so you are not to desire to be like the world. You should not to want what the world wants. Instead desire what the Lord desires for you. The children of Israel wanted someone to lead them like the surrounding nations. They already had God, but felt like he wasn't enough for them.

May you learn to be satisfied with the spiritual leader that God has given you. If you begin feeling like you know more than your leaders, you are in the wrong house. Be kind enough to dismiss yourself and leave because God is not the author of confusion.

Saul Prays and Gets No Answer

"*Then Saul said, "Let us go down after the Philistines by night and plunder them until the morning light, and let us not leave a man of them [alive]." They said, "Do whatever seems good to you." Then the priest said, "Let us approach God here." Saul asked [counsel] of God, "Shall I go down after the Philistines? Will You hand them over to Israel?" But He did not answer him that day. Then Saul said, "Come here, all you who are leaders of the people, and let us find out how this sin [causing God's silence] happened today. For as the LORD lives, who saves Israel, for even if the guilt is in my son Jonathan, he shall most certainly die." But not one of all the people answered him.*

Then he said to all the Israelites, " You shall be on one side; I and my son Jonathan will be on the other side." The people said to Saul, "Do what seems good to you." Therefore, Saul said to the LORD, the God of Israel, "Give a perfect lot [identifying the transgressor]." Then Saul and Jonathan were selected [by lot], but the other men went free. Saul said, "Cast [lots] between me and my son Jonathan." And Jonathan was selected. Saul said to Jonathan, "Tell me what you have done." So Jonathan told him, "I tasted a little honey with the end of the staff that was in my hand. Here I am, I must die!" Saul answered, "May God do so [to me], and more also [if I do not keep my word], for you shall most certainly die, Jonathan." But the people said to Saul, "Must Jonathan, who has brought about this great victory in Israel, be put to death? Far from it! As the LORD lives, not one hair of his head shall fall to the ground, for he has worked with God this day." So the people rescued Jonathan and he was not put to death." – 1 Samuel 14:36-45 AMP

When you are inquiring of the Lord and He doesn't answer your prayers, take a step back and see if you can determine where the fault lies. It could be that repentance is needed or that something has been done that has forced God's hand to withdraw from you. Whatever it is, try to rectify it. Don't allow it to remain unfixed. The situation with Saul and Jonathan was something that should have been handled in a much better way. What had been done by Jonathan was not deserving of death, so before we write someone off because they haven't completely given up everything, know that the blood of Jesus still works and it still covers all sin, not some sin but all sin. That person's turnaround is coming intercessor. Just watch and wait it's coming.

Samuel Travails In Prayer Over Saul

"Then the word of the LORD came to Samuel, saying, "I regret that I made Saul king, for he has turned away from following Me and has not carried out My commands." Samuel was angry [over Saul's failure] and he cried out to the LORD all night. When Samuel got up early in the morning to meet Saul, he was told, "Saul came to Carmel, and behold, he set up for himself a monument [commemorating his victory], then he turned and went on and went down to Gilgal.""

- 1 Samuel 15:10-12 AMP

David Prays to the Lord for Guidance

"Then they told David, saying, "Behold, the Philistines are fighting against Keilah and are plundering (robbing) the threshing floors [of the grain]." So David inquired of the LORD, saying, "Shall I go and attack these Philistines?" And the Lord said to David, "Go and attack the Philistines and save Keilah." But David's men said to him, "Listen, we are afraid here in Judah. How much more then if we go to Keilah against the battle lines of the Philistines?" Then David inquired of the LORD again. And the LORD answered him, "Arise, go down to Keilah, for I will hand over the Philistines to you." So David and his men went to Keilah and fought the Philistines; he drove away their cattle and struck them with a great slaughter. So David rescued the inhabitants of Keilah. When Abiathar the son of Ahimelech fled to David at Keilah, he came down with an ephod in his hand. Now when Saul was informed that David had come to Keilah, Saul said, "God has handed him over to me, for he shut himself in by entering a city that has double gates and bars." So Saul summoned all the people (soldiers) for war, to go down to Keilah to besiege David and his men. But David knew that Saul was plotting evil against him; and he said to Abiathar the priest, "Bring the ephod here."

Then David said, "O LORD, the God of Israel, Your servant has heard for certain that Saul intends to come to Keilah, to destroy the city on my account. Will the men of Keilah hand me over to him? Will Saul come down just as Your servant has heard? O LORD, God of Israel, I pray, tell Your servant." And the LORD said, "He will come down." Then David asked, "Will the men of Keilah surrender me and my men to Saul?" The LORD said, "They will surrender you. "Then David and his men, about six hundred, arose and left Keilah, and they went wherever they could go. When Saul was told that David had escaped from Keilah, he gave up the pursuit. David stayed in the wilderness in strongholds, in the hill country of the Wilderness of Ziph. Saul searched for him every day, but God did not hand David over to him." – 1 Samuel 23:1-14AMP

Just as David prayed for guidance, so should you. There is nothing wrong with consulting God concerning what you should be doing, especially if you're not sure. Seek God's wise counsel, He will never steer you wrong. If there is something that you desire to do and all of the particulars are not known, be like David and inquire. I've never known God to give a wrong answer. Before David and his men pursued after their enemy, David asked God about the enemy. Are you asking God about what your next move should be? You may have people with you that don't have the faith in God that you have. It doesn't make them bad people it's just good to know the people that are in your ranks and who you have walking beside you.

  You may have a Saul on your trail waiting to take your life but know that Saul could not take David's life because God had not given Saul permission. Your enemy may have permission to fight against you but that's to strengthen your fight not to take your life. Your enemy may be in hot pursuit of you, but God will always keep you out of the enemies clutches. He will not allow those that you have fought for to turn you over to the enemy.

- 1 Samuel 15:10-12 AMP

The Lord Doesn't Answer Saul

"The Philistines assembled and came and camped at Shunem; and Saul gathered all the Israelites and they camped at Gilboa. When Saul saw the Philistine army, he was afraid and badly shaken. So Saul inquired of the LORD, but the LORD did not answer him, either by dreams or by Urim [used like lots by the priest to determine the will of God] or by prophets."

- 1 Samuel 28:4-6 AMP

Intercessors always remember that it's bad to be in a position where you need God to speak, and He doesn't say a word. Saul had pursued after David relentlessly. He even had the priests of the Lord killed because they gave David and his men bread and the sword of Goliath. Once God takes his hands off of you, it's like a free for all. Fear and every other spirit you have opened the door to will replace the peace of God. Examine your heart to make sure that your will and desires are God's will and His desires. Close every door of disobedience that keeps you from fully obeying God.

David Inquires of God Regarding the Raid on Ziklag

"Now it happened when David and his men came [home] to Ziklag on the third day, [they found] that the Amalekites had made a raid on the Negev (the South country) and on Ziklag, and had overthrown Ziklag and burned it with fire; and they had taken captive the women [and all] who were there, both small and great. They killed no one, but carried them off [to be used as slaves] and went on their way. When David and his men came to the town, it was burned, and their wives and their sons and their daughters had been taken captive. Then David

and the people who were with him raised their voices and wept until they were too exhausted to weep [any longer]. Now David's two wives had been captured, Ahinoam the Jezreelitess and Abigail the widow of Nabal the Carmelite. Further, David was greatly distressed because the people spoke of stoning him, for all of them were embittered, each man for his sons and daughters. But David felt strengthened and encouraged in the LORD his God. David said to Abiathar the priest, Ahimelech's son, "Please bring me the ephod." So Abiathar brought him the ephod. David inquired of the LORD, saying, "Shall I pursue this band [of raiders]? Will I overtake them?" And He answered him, "Pursue, for you will certainly overtake them, and you will certainly rescue [the captives]."" – 1 Samuel 30:1-8 AMP

Seek the counsel of the Lord God concerning the matters that concern you. He will instruct you on whether or not you should deal with it now or wait and deal with it at another time. God will never leave you without counsel. David inquired. He needed guidance. The men were upset and wanted to kill him, but he encouraged himself in the Lord just as you should do, as often as you need to.

"In everything give thanks; for this is the will of God in Christ Jesus for you." - 1 Thessalonians 5:18 NKJV

Chapter Nine

The Book of 2 Samuel

David Inquires About His Next Move

"So it happened after this that David inquired of the LORD, saying, "Shall I go up into one of the cities of Judah?" And the LORD said to him, "Go up." David asked, "Where shall I go?" And He said, "To Hebron." So David went up there [to Hebron] with his two wives also, Ahinoam of Jezreel and Abigail the widow of Nabal of Carmel [in Judah]. And David brought up his men who were with him, each one with his household; and they lived in the cities of Hebron. – 2 Samuel 2:1-3 AMP

Intercessors we see David inquiring of the Lord concerning where he should move. He wanted to know if it was the appointed time to move to one of the cities in Judah and God told him to go up. David asked which one and God replied, "Hebron."

Before you launch out to start a new business, purchase a bigger edifice or to ordain new sons or daughters, inquire of the Lord and He will give you the specifics. He may not give it to you all at once, but little by little He will make his will known to you.

David Blesses the Men of Jabesh-Gilead

"Then the men of Judah came and there they anointed David king over the house of Judah. Then they told David, "It was the men of Jabesh-gilead who buried Saul." So David sent messengers to the men of Jabesh-gilead, and said to them, "May you be blessed by the LORD because you showed this

graciousness and loyalty to Saul your lord (king), and buried him. Now may the LORD show lovingkindness and truth and faithfulness to you. I too will show this goodness to you, because you have done this thing. So now, let your hands be strong and be valiant; for your lord Saul is dead, and also the house of Judah has anointed me king over them.""
– 2 Samuel 2:4-7 AMP

David blesses the men of Jabesh-Gilead because of their kindness to Saul and his sons after their death. There is nothing wrong with being a blessing to someone God has placed on your heart to bless. What a powerful example by David to remember the sacrifices of others and when it's in your power to bless them, to do just that, no questions asked.

David Prays for Counsel

"When the Philistines heard that David had been anointed king over Israel, all the Philistines went up to look for him, but he heard about it and went down to the stronghold. Now the Philistines had come and spread out [for battle] in the Valley of Rephaim. David inquired of the LORD, saying, "Shall I go up against the Philistines? Will You hand them over to me?" And the LORD said to David, "Go up, for I will certainly hand them over to you." So David came to Baal-perazim, and he defeated them there, and said, "The LORD has broken through my enemies before me, like a breakthrough of water." So he named that place Baal-perazim (master of breakthroughs). The Philistines abandoned their [pagan] idols there, so David and his men took them away [to be burned]. The Philistines came up once again and spread out in the Valley of Rephaim. When David inquired of the LORD, He said, "You shall not go up, but circle around behind them and come at them in front of the balsam trees. And when you hear the sound of marching in the

tops of the balsam trees, then you shall pay attention and act promptly, for at that time the LORD will have gone out before you to strike the army of the Philistines." David did just as the LORD had commanded him, and struck down the Philistines from Geba as far as Gezer." – 2 Samuel 5:17-25 AMP

When the enemy gets word about the great and mighty things that God has done for you, and they assemble themselves to fight against you, don't fear. Instead ask for counsel. There are battles that you will have to fight, but there are others that God will fight on your behalf. In the battles that you have to fight, ask God how you should assemble yourself for that battle. God may say fasting along with your intercession will get the job done. Whatever he says to you, be strategic about it and obey Him completely as you follow His leading.

    Once you have fought the adversary, know that you will always have some that want to prove they are better than you. So when the enemy comes the second, third, fourth or fifth time, don't fret. Know that God has a strategy to be used by you against them, and He will strike them down and you will witness their defeat.

David's Prayer of Gratitude

"Then King David went in and sat [in prayer] before the LORD, and said, "Who am I, O Lord GOD, and what is my house (family), that You have brought me this far? Yet this was very insignificant in Your eyes, O Lord GOD, for You have spoken also of Your servant's house (royal dynasty) in the distant future. And this is the law and custom of man, O Lord GOD. What more can David say to You? For You know (acknowledge, choose) Your servant, O Lord GOD. Because of Your word (promise), and in accordance with Your own heart, You have done all these great and astounding things to let Your

servant know (understand). Therefore You are great, O Lord GOD; for there is none like You, and there is no God besides You, according to all that we have heard with our ears. What one nation on earth is like Your people Israel, whom God went to redeem for Himself as a people and to make a name for Himself, and to do great and awesome things for Yourself and for Your land, before Your people whom You have redeemed for Yourself from Egypt, from nations and their gods? You established for Yourself Your people Israel as Your people forever, and You, O LORD, have become their God. Now, O LORD God, confirm forever the word [of the covenant] that You have spoken in regard to Your servant and his house (royal dynasty); and do just as You have spoken, so that Your Name may be magnified forever, saying, 'The LORD of hosts (armies) is God over Israel;' and may the house (royal dynasty) of Your servant David be established before You. For You, O LORD of hosts, God of Israel, have revealed this to Your servant, saying, 'I will build you a house (royal dynasty).' For that reason Your servant has found courage to pray this prayer to You. And now, O Lord GOD, You are God, and Your words are truth, and You have promised this good thing to Your servant. Therefore now, may it please You to bless the house (royal dynasty) of Your servant, so that it may continue forever before You; for You, O Lord GOD, have spoken it, and with Your blessing may the house of Your servant be blessed forever.''" – 2 Samuel 7:18-29 AMP

When God chose David, the baby of all his brothers, to be king, David was grateful. When God spoke to him about his future and what was to come, he was grateful. When God began performing the word that He had promised to him, David was beyond grateful. David took to acknowledge the accomplishments of the Lord. He magnified and glorified the name of the Lord. David makes mention of the things that God had done on behalf of Israel as well.

    Let's learn to be more grateful than we have been. Remind God of every promise that He made to you and how He was faithful and kept His word. When he makes known to you your future, give Him the praise. When He causes your enemies to be turned back from you and they stumble and fall, be grateful to Him for his mighty acts. As He heals your body, and it may be a gradual healing and not instantaneous, be grateful. Learn how to say, "God, thank you for all that you have done."

David Appeals for the Child's Life

"Then Nathan went [back] to his home. And the LORD struck the child that Uriah's widow bore to David, and he was very sick. David therefore appealed to God for the child [to be healed]; and David fasted and went in and lay all night on the ground. The elders of his household stood by him [in the night] to lift him up from the ground, but he was unwilling [to get up] and would not eat food with them. Then it happened on the seventh day that the child died. David's servants were afraid to tell him that the child was dead, for they said, "While the child was still alive, we spoke to him and he would not listen to our voices. How then can we tell him the child is dead, since he might harm himself [or us]?" But when David saw that his servants were whispering to one another, he realized that the child was dead. So David said to them, "Is the child dead?" And they said, "He is dead." Then David got up from the ground, washed, anointed himself [with olive oil], changed his clothes, and went into the house of the LORD and worshiped. Then he came [back] to his own house, and when he asked, they set food before him and he ate. Then his servants said to him, "What is this thing that you have done? While the child was alive you fasted and wept, but when the child died, you got up and ate

food." David said, "While the child was still alive, I fasted and wept; for I thought, 'Who knows, the LORD may be gracious to me and the child may live.' But now he is dead; why should I [continue to] fast? Can I bring him back again? I will go to him [when I die], but he will not return to me.""
-2 Samuel 12:15-23 AMP

Just as David fasted and prayed for the life of his child, and the child still died, you must learn to be like David and accept the perfect and divine will of God for your life. Learn to accept His will when it doesn't look like it's working for your good, when it's the total opposite of what you are praying for, when you have waited a long time and it seems like He has forgotten the promises He made, and when what you are facing seems to be unbearable. Let His will be done in your life.

"Saying, "Father, if it is Your will, take this cup away from Me; nevertheless not My will, but Yours, be done."" - Luke 22:42

David Laments for Absalom

"The king asked the Cushite, "Is the young man Absalom [my son] safe?" The Cushite replied, "May the enemies of my lord the king, and all those who rise against you to do evil, be [dead] like that young man is." The king was deeply moved and went to the upper room over the gate and wept [in sorrow]. And this is what he said as he walked: "O my son Absalom, my son, my son Absalom! How I wish that I had died instead of you, O Absalom, my son, my son!"" – 2 Samuel 18:32-33 AMP

Absalom, the son of David, not only wanted his father's throne, but his life as well. When Absalom was killed, we see David lamenting over his death, the son who had become his enemy.

David Is Reproved

"It was told to Joab, "Behold, the king is weeping and mourning for Absalom." So the victory on that day was turned into mourning for all the people, for the people heard it said on that day, "The king grieves for his son." The people stole into the city [of Mahanaim] that day, as people who are humiliated and ashamed steal away when they retreat in battle. But the king covered his face and cried out with a loud voice, "O my son Absalom, O Absalom, my son, my son!" Then Joab came into the house to the king and said, "Today you have put all your servants to shame who this day have saved your life and the lives of your sons and your daughters, and the lives of your wives and concubines. For you love those who hate you and hate those who love you. For you have shown today that commanders and servants are nothing to you; for today I know that if Absalom had lived and all the rest of us had died today, then you would be pleased. So now stand up, go out and speak kindly and encouragingly to your servants; for I swear by the LORD that if you do not go out, not a man will stay with you tonight. And this will be worse for you than all the evil that has come upon you from your youth until now.""

– 2 Samuel 19:1-7 AMP

Joab receives word that David is grieving over his son and the people are ashamed, so Joab confronts the king concerning his actions and he tells him he has put everyone to shame because of how he is acting. Intercessors, you must be careful not to cry over a dead thing. It could be an old season that you find yourself holding on to, let it go. It's been dead for a while, so why don't you bury it? People have left and you're still remembering what used to happen, what we used to do, and the fun times we used to have together. You are so caught up with the dead, that you don't see the living. Let it go. Man of God and woman of God, it's dead, so bury it. Holding on to it will only contaminate your future and keep you from moving forward. You don't need to be where God was, you need to be where God is.

Gibeonite Retribution

"There was famine in the days of David for three consecutive years; and David sought the presence (face) of the LORD [asking the reason]. The LORD replied, "It is because of Saul and his bloody house, because he put the Gibeonites to death." So the king called the Gibeonites and spoke to them (now the Gibeonites were not of the sons (descendants) of Israel but of the remnant (survivors) of the Amorites. The Israelites had sworn [an oath] to [spare] them, but Saul in his zeal for the sons of Israel and Judah had sought to strike down the Gibeonites). So David said to the Gibeonites, "What should I do for you? How can I make it good so that you will bless the LORD ' S inheritance (Israel)?" The Gibeonites said to him, "We will not accept silver or gold belonging to Saul or his household (descendants); nor is it for us to put any man to death in Israel." David said, "I will do for you whatever you say." So they said to the king, "The man who consumed us and planned to exterminate us from remaining in any territory of Israel, let seven men [chosen] from his sons (descendants) be given to us and we will hang them before the LORD [that is, put them on display, impaled with broken legs and arms] in Gibeah of Saul, the chosen one of the LORD." And the king said, "I will give them." But the king spared Mephibosheth the son of Jonathan, the son of Saul, because of the LORD ' S oath that was between David and Saul's son Jonathan. So the king took the two sons of Rizpah the daughter of Aiah, whom she bore to Saul, Armoni and Mephibosheth, and the five sons of

Merab the daughter of Saul, whom she had borne to Adriel the son of Barzillai the Meholathite. He handed them over to the Gibeonites, and they hanged them on the hill before the LORD, and the seven died together. They were put to death in the first days of the grain harvest, the beginning of the barley harvest [in the spring]." – 2 Samuel 21:1-9 AMP

Have you ever had to deal with a situation like this? One where something has transpired and you didn't have a clue where it originated from, but after praying and seeking the Lord's face for an answer, you find out that your predecessor has done something so despicable that you have to take the initiative to rectify the matter. So you go and talk with the person that has been wronged and you set about trying to fix the matter. In situations like this, knowing the voice of God is so important. David knew that something was wrong, he just didn't know what. Like him, you may sometimes feel that something is not right, but if you inquire of the Lord, the reason will be revealed and it will be up to you what you do with the information.

David's Song of Thanksgiving

Read David's Song of Thanksgiving in 2 Samuel 22:1-51. After reading it in its entirety, this should push your praise and worship to another level. When God delivers you from your enemies, you should make known all that He has done for you. If He is your rock, then say so. If He is your fortress and the God that has rescued you, make His name glorious. When you call on the Lord in your time of trouble and distress and He hears and answers you, give Him the praise. When God comes through and delivers you out of the grip of death, you should bless Him. As God continues to keep you safe from your enemy and from those who hate you, open your mouth and bless Him for who He is. When God doesn't allow your foot to slip, and He keeps you in all of your ways because you have kept yourself from doing wrong, magnify His name. As God continues to save you from every plot, plan and attack of the enemy, always remember that you have the strength to run through a troop and leap over a wall.

God will continue to set you on high places. He is your shield and you can trust in Him. He has trained your hands to war and your fingers to fight. He has equipped you for what is to come your way. Continue to honor Him for all that He has done. Continue to lift up His most holy name. He has surrounded you with more strength than you ever thought you had. Intercessor, continue to pursue after the enemy until they are destroyed. They will flee from before you because your God fights for you. The Lord lives and you should bless Him because He is the rock of your salvation, and He is your tower and your great deliverer.

David's Sin and Intercession

"But David's heart (conscience) troubled him after he had counted the people. David said to the LORD, "I have sinned greatly in what I have done. But now, O LORD, please take away the sin of Your servant, for I have acted very foolishly." When David got up in the morning, the word of the LORD came to the prophet Gad, David's seer, saying, "Go and say to David, 'Thus says the LORD, "I am giving you three choices; select one of them for yourself, and I will do it to you."'" So Gad came to David and told him, and said to him, "Shall seven years of famine come to you in your land? Or will you flee three months before your enemies as they pursue you? Or shall there be three days of pestilence (plague) in your land? Now consider this and decide what answer I shall return to Him

who sent me." Then David said to Gad, "I am in great distress. Let us fall into the hands of the LORD, for His mercies are great, but do not let me fall into the hands of man." So the LORD sent a pestilence (plague) [lasting three days] upon Israel from the morning until the appointed time, and seventy thousand men of the people from Dan to Beersheba died. When the [avenging] angel stretched out his hand toward Jerusalem to destroy it, the LORD relented from the disaster and said to the angel who destroyed the people, "It is enough! Now relax your hand." And the angel of the LORD was by the threshing floor of Araunah the Jebusite. When David saw the angel who was striking down the people, he spoke to the LORD and said, "Behold, I [alone] am the one who has sinned and done wrong; but these sheep (people of Israel), what have they done [to deserve this]? Please let Your hand be [only] against me and my father's house (family)."" – 2 Samuel 24:10-17 AMP

Intercessors, we have all sinned and done foolish things, but when the wrong that you have done comes before you, repent. Yes, there will be consequences for your actions, but repent and turn quickly back to the Lord. Acknowledge where you went wrong and repent. Cry out to the Lord for His mercy. Cry out to Him so that you will never make the same mistake twice. How God handled David in this matter should make us all tread carefully and reverently before God. David did something that he should not have done and once it was over his conscience got the best of him. So God sends the prophet Gad, David's seer to him, letting him know that I set before you three things, so the choice is up to you which one I shall do to you. David acknowledges his distress just as we should do when God tells us that we must pay for the wrong that we have done. Just as David says, "Let us fall into the hands of the Lord," hear me very well, just fall on the mercies of the Lord and allow him to deal with you right where you are. Your repentant heart can often times avert further calamity and cause God to say it is enough.

David Erects An Altar and Intercession Is Made for the Land

"Then Gad [the prophet] came to David that day and said to him, "Go up, set up an altar to the LORD on the threshing floor of Araunah the Jebusite [where you saw the angel]." So David went up according to Gad's word, as the LORD commanded. Araunah looked down and saw the king and his servants crossing over toward him; and he went out and bowed before the king with his face toward the ground. Araunah said, "Why has my lord the king come to his servant?" And David said, "To buy the threshing floor from you, to build an altar to the LORD, so that the plague may be held back from the people." Araunah said to David, "Let my lord the king take and offer up whatever seems good to him. Look, here are oxen for the burnt offering, and threshing sledges and the yokes of the oxen for the wood. All of this, O king, Araunah gives to the king." And Araunah said to the king, "May the LORD your God be favorable to you." But the king said to Araunah, "No, but I will certainly buy it from you for a price. I will not offer burnt offerings to the LORD my God which cost me nothing." So David purchased the threshing floor and the oxen for fifty shekels of silver. David built an altar to the LORD there, and offered burnt offerings and peace offerings. So the LORD was moved [to compassion] by [David's] prayer for the land, and the plague was held back from Israel."
- 2 Samuel 24:18-25 AMP

Intercessors, God will send a messenger to you. It could come through a vision or dream, but when it comes it is to instruct you on how to get back on the path called straight. God will send a voice that you can trust to direct you in what your next move should be, so that whatever price has to be paid, may be paid so that disaster can be turned back from you and those who are attached to you. Do it. Offer it willingly to Him as you intercede for those who are close to you, and who may suffer unknowingly because of your foolish acts. Give God what He desires and He will be moved with pity on you and relent.

"The sacrifices of God are a broken spirit, A broken and a contrite heart- These, O God, You will not despise."
– Psalm 51:17 NKJV

Chapter Ten

The Book of 1 Kings

Solomon's Prayer

"In Gibeon the LORD appeared to Solomon in a dream at night; and God said, "Ask [Me] what I shall give you." Then Solomon said, "You have shown Your servant David my father great lovingkindness, because he walked before You in faithfulness and righteousness and with uprightness of heart toward You; and You have kept for him this great lovingkindness, in that You have given him a son to sit on his throne, as it is today. So now, O LORD my God, You have made Your servant king in place of David my father; and as for me, I am but a little boy [in wisdom and experience]; I do not know how to go out or come in [that is, how to conduct business as a king]. Your servant is among Your people whom You have chosen, a great people who are too many to be numbered or counted. So give Your servant an understanding mind and a hearing heart [with which] to judge Your people, so that I may discern between good and evil. For who is able to judge and rule this great people of Yours?""

- 1 Kings 3:5-9 AMP

God came to Solomon in a dream at night and asked him what shall I give you? This is so awesome because God still communicates like this. Even now He will visit you while you are resting and converse with you and share with you concerning His movements in the earth realm as well as in the heavenly realm. Solomon is speaking to God and sharing his heart with Him. He begins reminiscing about the things that had been done by God for his father, David. Solomon says, "You love my father so much, that you allowed me, his son, to reign in his place. I am a little boy and I don't really know what I'm doing. You have placed me over your people who are too numerous to count, so give me an understanding heart so that I can judge your people. I want to be able to discern between good and evil." Wow, to have God visit you and ask you what can he do for you is pretty remarkable, but it does happen. To know that even while you are asleep you are praying is just as incredible. Whether asleep or awake, when God says pray without ceasing, you should definitely pray without ceasing. Intercessors, let's pray like Solomon and tell God that we need an understanding heart and that we want to be able to discern between good and evil. In the times in which we are living we need all the help that we can get, so ask, it's your right.

God Responds to the Prayer of Solomon

"Now it pleased the Lord that Solomon had asked this thing. God said to him, "Because you have asked this and have not asked for yourself a long life nor for wealth, nor for the lives of your enemies, but have asked for yourself understanding to recognize justice, behold, I have done as you asked. I have given you a wise and discerning heart (mind), so that no one before you was your equal, nor shall anyone equal to you arise after you. I have also given you what you have not asked, both wealth and honor, so that there will not be anyone equal to you among the kings, for all your days. If you walk in My ways, keeping My statutes and My commandments, as your father David did, then I will lengthen your days." Then Solomon awoke, and he realized that it was a dream. He came [back] to Jerusalem and stood before the ark of the covenant of the LORD; he offered burnt offerings and peace offerings, and he prepared a feast for all his servants." -1 Kings 3:10-15 AMP

Intercessors, this passage of scripture says that God was pleased that Solomon asked for this thing. This let's me know that it's okay to ask God to give it to you, for He desires to give you the best of everything that He has so that your walk before Him can be one of strength, power and authority. Intercessors there is no need to ask for the life of your enemies, God has that taken care of. God will give you long life and riches untold, but these things should not be your main focus. An understanding heart to be able to discern good from evil is what you should ask for.

Solomon's Dedication and Prayer

"Then Solomon stood [in the courtyard] before the altar of the LORD in the presence of all the assembly of Israel and spread out his hands toward heaven. He said, "O LORD, the God of Israel, there is no God like You in heaven above or on earth below, who keeps the covenant and shows lovingkindness to Your servants who walk before You with all their heart; You who have kept what You promised to Your servant my father David. You have spoken with Your mouth and have fulfilled Your word with Your hand, as it is this day. Now therefore, O LORD, the God of Israel, keep for Your servant my father David that which You promised him when You said, 'You shall not be without a man (descendant) to sit on the throne of Israel, if only your sons take heed to their way [of life] to walk before Me [according to my laws] as you have done.' Now, O God of Israel, please let Your word which You have spoken to Your servant David my father be confirmed. But will God indeed dwell on the earth? Behold, heaven and the highest heaven cannot contain You; how much less this house which I have built! Yet graciously consider the prayer of Your servant and his supplication, O LORD my God, to listen to the [loud] cry and to the prayer which Your servant prays before You

today; that Your eyes may be open toward this house night and day, toward the place of which You have said, 'My Name (Presence) shall be there,' that You may listen to the prayer which Your servant shall pray toward this place. Listen to the prayer of Your servant and of Your people Israel which they pray toward this place. Hear in heaven, Your dwelling place; hear and forgive. "If a man sins against his neighbor and is made to take an oath [of innocence] and he comes to take the oath before Your altar in this house (temple), then hear from heaven and act and judge Your servants, condemning the wicked by bringing his guilt on his own head, and justifying the righteous by rewarding him in accordance with his righteousness." -1 Kings 8:22-32 AMP

After twenty years, the temple has finally been completed and Solomon is now ready to offer the dedication and one of at least nine prayers. As Solomon stands before the altar of the Lord, I can only imagine how honored he must have felt that God had chosen him over all of his brothers to build God a house. So lifting his hands towards the heavens, Solomon acknowledges that there is no God like the God of Israel in heaven above or in the earth beneath who keeps His promises. I can literally feel Solomon's excitement at having accomplished so great a task, especially when there were many others in the midst that felt that they were more qualified than he was. Nevertheless, the God of his father David had been faithful and had chosen him above all others.

    Intercessors, God may have called you to build and there are those around you that feel you are too young or that you don't have enough experience, but know that if God is for you, He is more than the world against you. The same God that Solomon honored is the same God that you honor now. It's alright to bless the Lord and make declarations about Him being a God who keeps His promises. People need to know that the God you serve always keeps His promises and never fails. As massive as we know the heavens to be, they cannot contain all that the Lord God from everlasting to everlasting is. I thank God that we can follow Solomon's example and no matter how daunting the task may seem, as we push to complete things that He has asked of us, He will hear us when we pray.

Solomon's Second Prayer

""When Your people Israel are defeated before an enemy because they have sinned against You, and then they turn to You again and praise Your Name and pray and ask for Your favor and compassion in this house (temple), then hear in heaven, and forgive the sin of Your people Israel, and bring them back to the land which You gave their fathers."
–1 Kings 8:33-34 AMP

Solomon was the kind of leader that believed in intercessory prayer. His intercession was so detailed and precise that notes should be taken on how he covered the congregation in prayer as he stood and knelt before the people. He prayed concerning the people being defeated by their enemies because of sin against God and what the outcome would be for them if they were to turn back to God. Just like Solomon, as intercessors we should pray and ask for God's favor and compassion.

Solomon's Third Prayer

""When the heavens are shut up and there is no rain because they have sinned against You, and they pray toward this place and praise Your name and turn from their sin when You afflict them, then hear in heaven and forgive the sin of Your servants

and of Your people Israel; indeed, teach them the good way in which they should walk (live). And send rain on Your land which You have given to Your people as an inheritance."

- 1 Kings 8:35-36 AMP

Even after this third prayer, Solomon continues to pray and seek the face of God. What an awesome example we see in this leader who intercedes for all people. Once he finishes praying, he stands before the people and pronounces a blessing saying, "Blessed be God who has given you peace and nothing that he has spoken has failed to come to pass. May he continue to lead and guide us as he led and guided those who were before me. May God never leave us or abandon us and may our hearts be guided by him, may the prayers that I have prayed always be before him so that everyone everywhere may know that the Lord is God so walk before him in full devotion always keeping his commandments."

God Answers Solomon's Prayers of Dedication

"Now it happened when Solomon had finished building the house (temple) of the LORD and the king's house (palace), and all else which he was pleased to do, that the LORD appeared to Solomon a second time, just as He had appeared to him at Gibeon. The LORD told him, "I have heard your prayer and supplication which you have made before Me; I have consecrated this house which you have built by putting My Name and My Presence there forever. My eyes and My heart shall be there perpetually. As for you, if you walk (live your life) before Me, as David your father walked, in integrity of heart and in uprightness, acting in accordance with everything that I have commanded you, and will keep My statutes and My precepts, then I will establish the throne of your kingdom over Israel forever, just as I promised your father David,

saying, 'You shall not be without a man (descendant) on the throne of Israel.' "But if you or your sons turn away from following Me, and do not keep My commandments and My statutes which I have set before you, but go and serve other gods and worship them, then I will cut off Israel from the land which I have given them, and I will cast out of My sight the house which I have consecrated for My Name and Presence. Then Israel will become a proverb (a saying) and a byword (object of ridicule) among all the peoples. This house (temple) will become a heap of ruins; everyone who passes by will be appalled and sneer and say, 'Why has the LORD done such a thing to this land and to this house?' And they [who know] will say, 'Because they abandoned the LORD their God, who brought their fathers out of the land of Egypt, and they have chosen other gods and have worshiped and served them; that is the reason the LORD has brought on them all this adversity.""

- 1 Kings 9:1-9 AMP

The Lord appeared to Solomon a second time in a dream and tells him that he has heard and accepted his prayers. God then goes on to tell him that if he walks before Him, like his father David, in integrity of his heart, then his throne would be established and one of his sons would always sit on the throne; but if his sons turn away from doing His will and decide to serve other gods and worship them, then He would cut them off from the land and cast them out of it.

Intercessors, let's make sure that the life that we live before God is one of integrity and that we raise those that are in our homes to be people of integrity as well.

A Man of God From Judah Prays for Jeroboam

"Now behold, there came a man of God from Judah to Bethel by the word (command) of the LORD, while Jeroboam was standing by the altar [which he had built] to burn incense. The man cried out against the [idolatrous] altar by the word of the LORD, "O altar, altar, thus says the Lord: 'Behold, a son shall be born to the house of David, Josiah by name; and on you shall he sacrifice [the bodies of] the priests of the high places who burn incense on you, and human bones shall be burned on you.'" And he gave a sign the same day, saying, "This is the sign which the LORD has spoken: 'Behold, the altar shall be split apart and the ashes that are on it shall be poured out.'" When the king heard the words which the man of God cried out against the altar in Bethel, Jeroboam put out his hand from the altar, saying, "Seize him!" And his hand which he had put out against him withered, so that he was unable to pull it back to himself. The altar also was split apart and the ashes were poured out from the altar in accordance with the sign which the man of God had given by the word of the LORD. The king answered and said to the man of God, "Please entreat [the favor of] the LORD your God and pray for me, that my hand may be restored to me." So the man of God entreated the LORD, and the king's hand was restored to him and became as it was before." - 1 KINGS 13:1-6 AMP

God sends a man of God from Judah to Bethel to deliver a word to King Jeroboam. This stands out to me because he is not named, but God still used him. Often times we want to be known, but what if no one ever calls your name. Would you be find with that? Continuing on, Jeroboam stands by the altar that he has built when the man of God delivers a prophetic word to King Jeroboam concerning a son who would come through the lineage of David. His name would be Josiah and God would use him mightily to pull down and destroy the evil works that were being done on that altar. King Jeroboam becomes upset that the man of God released a word of correction and destruction, so he raises his hand and tells those that are around him to seize the man of God. At that moment the hand that was raised against the man of God withers and he is not able to pull it back.

Intercessors obey the word of the Lord God. If he sends you go, and whatever he tells you to say, say it.

"" Do not be afraid of their faces, For I am with you to deliver you," says the Lord."" – Jeremiah 1:8 NKJV

Jeroboam asks the man of God to pray for him so that his hand would be restored. He prayed and God listened. Jeroboam's hand was healed.

God may have given you a word for someone and maybe it wasn't a word that was received well and they became upset about the whole thing and may even have tried to harm you with their words, but use the man of God's example. They are going to need your intercession, so when they approach you just pray. Remember it's not about them, it's about you, remain a person of integrity.

Elijah Prays for the Widow's Son

"It happened after these things, that the son of the woman, the mistress of the house, became sick; and his illness was so severe that there was no breath left in him. So she said to Elijah, "What [problem] is there between you and me, O man of God? Have you come to me to bring my sin to mind and to put my son to death?" He said to her, "Give me your son." Then he took him from her arms and carried him up to the upper room where he was living, and laid him on his own bed. He called to the LORD and said, "O LORD my God, have You brought further tragedy to the widow with whom I am staying, by causing her son to die?" Then he stretched himself out upon the

child three times, and called to the LORD and said, "O LORD my God, please let this child's life return to him." The LORD heard the voice of Elijah, and the life of the child returned to him and he revived. Elijah took the child and brought him down from the upper room into the [lower part of the] house and gave him to his mother; and Elijah said, "See, your son is alive." Then the woman said to Elijah, "Now I know that you are a man of God and that the word of the LORD in your mouth is truth."" – 1 Kings 17:17-24 AMP

Elijah enters into intercession by first asking God if He brought him there to be a burden to the widow woman. He lies on the child three different times and says, "Please let this child's life be restored to him." God hears the voice of Elijah and answers his intercession on behalf of the child and his life is restored.

"Death and life are in the power of the tongue, And those who love it will eat its fruit." - Proverbs 18:21 NKJV

Like the Prophet Elijah, sometimes it's best to keep quiet and let the miracle speak for itself. The boy's mother could not deny that her son was dead but was now alive. Elijah used the power that was on the inside of him and commanded life to be restored back into the child. In this instance the miracle spoke for Elijah.

The Showdown With the 450 Prophets of Baal

In this passage, we see Elijah and the 450 prophets of Baal in the process of having a showdown. Elijah was definitely outnumbered in the natural, but he had God on his side. The prophets of Baal chose a bull and went into this whole routine that yielded no results. They screamed and hollered and even cut themselves and blood flowed freely, but still there was no answer. Elijah calls the people to him and he repairs the altar that had been torn down and takes twelve stones representing the twelve tribes of Israel, and builds a new altar in the name of the Lord. He then makes a trench around it. Elijah lays the wood on the altar, cuts an ox and lies it on the wood, and tells the water bearers to fill four pitchers with water and cover the burnt offering and the wood, and after they have done this to do it three more times so that the water will fill the trench as well.

God had given Elijah precise instructions and he followed every directive. Once it is time for the offering of the evening sacrifice, Elijah approaches the altar and begins to pray. He says, "Lord God let it be known on this day that you are God in Israel and that I serve you and everything that I have done is because you said do it, so I did. Now answer my prayers Lord, so that the people may know that you are still God in Israel and their hearts can fully return to you." Fire falls from the Lord and everything that Elijah had placed on the altar is instantaneously consumed. The people fall down on their faces and proclaim that the Lord is God.

Intercessors, you may be outnumbered in the battle naturally, but when you abide by what God says and pray it out the way He tells you to, then God will not only show up, but he will also accept your prayers.

Elijah Intercedes Until the Rain Falls

"So Ahab went up to eat and to drink. And Elijah went up to the top of Carmel; and he crouched down to the earth and put his face between his knees, and he said to his servant, "Go up, look toward the sea." So he went up and looked and said, "There is nothing." Elijah said, "Go back" seven times. And at the seventh time the servant said, "A cloud as small as a man's

hand is coming up from the sea." And Elijah said, "Go up, say to Ahab, 'Prepare your chariot and go down, so that the rain shower does not stop you.'" In a little while the sky grew dark with clouds and wind, and there were heavy showers. And Ahab mounted and rode [his chariot] and went [inland] to Jezreel. Then the hand of the LORD came upon Elijah [giving him supernatural strength]. He girded up his loins and outran Ahab to the entrance of Jezreel [nearly twenty miles]."
- 1 Kings 18:42-46 AMP

Elijah has gone up to the top of Carmel to pray for rain, so he gives his servant instructions to go up and when he gets there to look toward the sea. The servant goes and looks as Elijah instructed, and he comes back to Elijah and says, "There is nothing there." So Elijah tells him to go back. The servant goes a second time and there's nothing, and a third time, but still there's nothing. Each time the servant goes to look, he comes back with the same report. Through all of this Elijah's confidence in prayer never wavers. He stays true to the assignment and prays. The servant goes a fourth time, but still there is nothing there, a fifth time- still nothing there, and again a sixth time, but still there is nothing there. Inspite of this, Elijah remains steadfast in his assignment.

Therefore, my beloved brethren, be steadfast, immovable, always abounding in the work of the Lord, knowing that your labor is not in vain in the Lord. – 1 Corinthians 15:58 NKJV

Elijah sends his servant a seventh time, and finally he returns and says, "I see a cloud as small as a man's hand coming from the sea." Intercessors, what if Elijah had become discouraged and had stopped praying by the third or even the sixth time? He would not have seen God perform the miracle of the abundance of rain.

Elijah sends his servant to tell Ahab to prepare his chariot and to leave from where he is, so that the rain would not stop him. Ahab does as instructed and goes to Jezreel. The hand of the Lord comes upon Elijah supernaturally and he outruns Ahab to the entrance of Jezreel. Elijah had a job to do, just as you do. Intercession is a necessity. Elijah could have left Ahab where he was, but he didn't. He warned him about the upcoming rain, so that he would be could make it out as well. Let's not hold grudges. Just follow the leading of the Lord and pray.

Elijah Prays for Death

"And Elijah was afraid and arose and ran for his life, and he came to Beersheba which belongs to Judah, and he left his servant there. But he himself traveled a day's journey into the wilderness, and he came and sat down under a juniper tree and asked [God] that he might die. He said, "It is enough; now, O LORD, take my life, for I am no better than my fathers." He lay down and slept under the juniper tree, and behold, an angel touched him and said to him, "Get up and eat." He looked, and by his head there was a bread cake baked on hot coal, and a pitcher of water. So he ate and drank and lay down again. Then the angel of the LORD came again a second time and touched him and said, "Get up, and eat, for the journey is too long for you [without adequate sustenance]." So he got up and ate and drank, and with the strength of that food he traveled forty days and nights to Horeb (Sinai), the mountain of God."
- 1 Kings 19:3-8 AMP

We find Elijah in a major state of depression. He was so depressed that he prayed for God to kill him. He actually wanted to die. He felt hopeless and like there was nothing else for him. As he lay down and slept, God sent an angel to feed him, not once, but twice because he had to go on the strength of those two meals to Horeb for forty days and forty nights.

Intercessors, you may be dealing with depression like Elijah. Come out of agreement with depression and close the door to it. There is so much more work for you to do in the kingdom. There are people that are assigned only to you, and your intercession is needed to bring them out of darkness and into His marvelous light.

Chapter Eleven

The Book of 2 Kings

Elisha Prays and the Dead Son is Raised to Life

Read 2 Kings 4:25-37. In this passage of scripture the Shunammite woman comes to the prophet Elisha because her son has died. Elisha sees her in the distant and tells his servant Gehazi to see if all was well with her. She says that all is well, but once she arrives to where Elisha is, she grabs his feet. Gehazi attempts to push her away, but Elisha tells him to leave her alone because she is troubled and the Lord has hidden what is really going on with her. The woman tells Elisha that her son has died, so Elisha instructs Gehazi to take his staff and go the Shunammite woman's; and once he arrives to lay the staff on the child's face. Gehazi does as instructed. When Elisha and the woman arrive at the house, Elisha goes into the room where the child is and shuts the door behind them. He then begins to pray to the Lord, and lies on the child. The child's body begins to get warm and he walks around and returns and lies on him again and this time the child sneezes seven times before opening his eyes. Elisha tells Gehazi to call the Shunammite and he presents her son to her alive and well, and she bows at his feet in reverence.

Intercessors, Elisha could have given up when he came into the house and saw that the child was still dead after Gehazi had done as he was instructed. Ultimately, it took Elisha leaving his place of comfort to intercede over the child, to wrought this miracle.

As an intercessor, there are many times you will

have to leave your comfort zone to get the job done for the kingdom.

Elisha Prays for His Servant's Eyes to be Opened

"The servant of the man of God got up early and went out, and behold, there was an army with horses and chariots encircling the city. Elisha's servant said to him, "Oh no, my master! What are we to do?" Elisha answered, "Do not be afraid, for those who are with us are more than those who are with them." Then Elisha prayed and said, "LORD, please, open his eyes that he may see." And the LORD opened the servants eyes and he saw; and behold, the mountain was full of horses and chariots of fire surrounding Elisha." – 2 Kings 6:15-17 AMP

The servant of Elisha got up and went outside, and became frightened by the sight of an army with horses and chariots surrounding the city that they were in, so he goes and tells Elisha what he has seen and asks him what they are going to do? Elisha wanted his servant to see what he saw, so he prayed that God would open his eyes to see that the protection of the army of God was way more than he could even comprehend. God answered and opened his eyes; and he saw that the mountain was full of chariots and horses.

Intercessors that are reading this book, you may have those that are walking close to you whose faith needs to be elevated, pray that God will open their eyes that they may see that He is still working on your behalf.

Elisha Offers Prayers of Intercession and Faith

"When the Arameans came down to him, Elisha prayed to the LORD and said, "Please strike this people (nation) with blindness." And God struck them with blindness, in accordance

with Elisha's request. Then Elisha said to the Arameans, "This is not the way, nor is this the city. Follow me and I will lead you to the man whom you are seeking." And he led them to Samaria." – 2 Kings 6:18-19 AMP

As the army approached him, Elisha prayed in faith that God would strike them with blindness and God did just as he asked. Elisha did not pray that God would kill them dead or kill their children he just asked that their sight would be removed from them. We are instructed to pray for our enemies, so let's do that.

"But I say to you who hear: Love your enemies, do good to those who hate you, bless those who curse you, and pray for those who spitefully use you." - Luke 6:27-28 NKJV

Elisha Offers Prayers of Intercession and Faith Once More

"When they had come into Samaria, Elisha said, "LORD, open the eyes of these men, so that they may see." And the LORD opened their eyes and they saw. Behold, they were in the midst of Samaria." – 2 Kings 6:20 AMP

Elisha prayed in faith once again, but this time he prayed for their eyes to be opened; and the Lord answered. Continue to pray for those that you know to be your enemies, and watch how God turns that thing around on your behalf.

Hezekiah Offers Prayers

"Hezekiah received the letter from the hand of the messengers and read it. Then he went up to the house (temple) of the LORD and spread it out before the LORD. Hezekiah prayed before the LORD and said, "O LORD, the God of Israel, who is enthroned above the cherubim [of the ark in the temple], You are the God, You alone, of all the kingdoms of the earth. You have made the heavens and the earth. O LORD, bend down Your ear and hear; LORD, open Your eyes and see; hear the [taunting] words of Sennacherib, which he has sent to taunt and defy the living God. It is true, LORD, that the Assyrian kings have devastated the nations and their lands and have thrown their gods into the fire, for they were not [real] gods but [only] the work of men's hands, wood and stone. So they [could destroy them and] have destroyed them. Now, O LORD our God, please, save us from his hand so that all the kingdoms of the earth may know [without any doubt] that You alone, O LORD, are God."" – 2 Kings 19:14-19 AMP

Intercessors your prayers are needful even in times of trouble. With everything that is happening in our nation and around the world, we must cry out and intercede as Hezekiah did. We must cry out until God hears, moves and sends a solution because He will.

Hezekiah's Prayers Are Heard

"Then Isaiah the son of Amoz sent word to Hezekiah, saying, "Thus says the LORD, the God of Israel: 'I have heard your prayer to Me regarding Sennacherib king of Assyria.' This is the word that the LORD has spoken against him: 'The virgin daughter of Zion Has despised you and mocked you; The daughter of Jerusalem Has shaken her head behind you! 'Whom have you taunted and blasphemed? Against whom

have you raised your voice, And haughtily lifted up your eyes? Against the Holy One of Israel! ⁷*Through your messengers you have taunted and defied the Lord, And have said [boastfully], "With my many chariots I came up to the heights of the mountains, To the remotest parts of Lebanon; I cut down its tall cedar trees and its choicest cypress trees. I entered its most distant lodging, its densest forest.* *"I dug wells and drank foreign waters, And with the sole of my feet I dried up All the rivers of [the Lower Nile of] Egypt."* ⁸*'Have you not heard [asks the God of Israel]? Long ago I did it; From ancient times I planned it. Now I have brought it to pass, That you [king of Assyria] should [be My instrument to] turn fortified cities into ruinous heaps.* ⁹*Therefore their inhabitants were powerless, They were shattered [in spirit] and put to shame; They were like plants of the field, the green herb, As grass on the housetops is scorched before it is grown up.* ⁷*But I [the LORD] know your sitting down [O Sennacherib], Your going out, your coming in, And your raging against Me.* ⁸*Because of your raging against Me, And because your arrogance and complacency have come up to My ears, I will put My hook in your nose, And My bridle in your lips, And I will turn you back [to Assyria] by the way that you came."* – 2 Kings 19:20-28 AMP

God sends the prophet Isaiah to tell King Hezekiah that he has heard his intercession concerning his enemy. Isaiah brings words of comfort from God to Hezekiah, and assures him that God is going to deal with the matter. Intercessors, there may be people that you know, and they may have been sent by the enemy to hurl threats at you, but don't you fear. Stay on the wall and don't come down. God is about to disrupt the plans of the enemy concerning you.

Hezekiah Prays for His Own Healing

"In those days [when Sennacherib first invaded Judah] Hezekiah became deathly ill. The prophet Isaiah the son of Amoz came and said to him, "Thus says the LORD, 'Set your house in order, for you shall die and not recover.'" Then Hezekiah turned his face to the wall and prayed to the LORD, saying, "Please, O LORD, remember now [with compassion] how I have walked before You in faithfulness and truth and with a whole heart [entirely devoted to You], and have done what is good in Your sight." And Hezekiah wept bitterly. Before Isaiah had gone out of the middle courtyard, the word of the LORD came to him, saying, "Go back and tell Hezekiah the leader of My people, 'Thus says the LORD, the God of David your father (ancestor): "I have heard your prayer, I have seen your tears. Behold, I am healing you; on the third day you shall go up to the house of the LORD. I will add fifteen years to your life and save you and this city [Jerusalem] from the hand of the king of Assyria; and I will protect this city for My own sake and for My servant David's sake." - 2 Kings 20:1-6 AMP

Hezekiah has become sick unto death, so God sends the prophet Isaiah to him and says, "Get your house in order, you are about to die" Hezekiah turns his face to the wall and begins to petition God for himself, reminding God of the things that He had done. Before Isaiah even makes it through the middle court, God makes him turn around and go back to Hezekiah to tell him that his petitions for himself have been heard and that God is going to heal him, and on the third day he would be able to go up to the house of the Lord and he was adding an additional fifteen years to his life.

Just like Hezekiah, there is nothing wrong with praying for yourself; and there is nothing wrong with talking to God about you. You take others to him, now take yourself. Pour your needs and desires out to him. If you're sick, tell him. If there are things that you need, He is your source.

Hilkiah Sent On A Mission By the King

"Now when the king heard the words of the Book of the Law, he tore his clothes. Then the king commanded Hilkiah the priest, Ahikam the son of Shaphan, Achbor the son of Micaiah, Shaphan the scribe, and Asaiah the servant of the king, saying, "Go, inquire of the LORD for my sake and for the sake of the people and for all Judah concerning the words of this book which has been found, for great is the wrath of the LORD which has been kindled against us, because our fathers have not listened to and obeyed the words of this book, so as to act in accordance with everything that is written concerning us.""

- 2 Kings 22:11-13 AMP

The book of the law had been presented and read to King Josiah and when he heard the words of the book he tore his clothes and gave a command to Hilkiah the priest and Ahikam, Achbor, Micaiah, Shapan the scribe and Asaiah the servant of the Josiah saying to them, "Go and inquire of the Lord for me, the people and for all of Judah because the wrath of the Lord is coming because our fathers have not been obedient to the words of the book."

Intercessors, just like Josiah, when you inherit something and you later find out that what you are dealing with needs to be fixed, then there is nothing wrong with inquiring of the Lord's wisdom and counsel concerning the matter. Go to those that you trust. You can't go to everyone, so be led by God to a man or woman of God of integrity who can see what you don't see and hear what you cannot hear.

Huldah the Prophetess Has the Answer

"But to the king of Judah who sent you to inquire of the LORD, you shall say this to him: 'Thus says the LORD God of Israel, " Regarding the words which you have heard, because your heart was tender (receptive, penitent) and you humbled yourself before the LORD when you heard what I said against this place and against its inhabitants, that they should become a desolation and a curse, and because you have torn your clothes and wept before Me, I have heard you," declares the LORD. "Therefore, behold, [King Josiah,] I will gather you to your fathers, and you will be taken to your grave in peace, and your eyes will not see all the evil (catastrophe) which I will bring on this place." So they brought back word to the king."
- 2 Kings 22:18-20 AMP

Hilkiah and the men that were with him went to Huldah the prophetess who had a word for King Josiah from the Lord. The Lord wanted the king to know that he had seen the tenderness of his heart and how he humbled himself before the Lord when he heard what God was about to do to the city and it's people. Intercessors I told you before, God will give you people of integrity, who can see and hear for you. They will not give you a tainted word. It will be truth. God wants you to know that like Josiah your tears have come up before him intercessor and the way of escape for you has already been made.

Chapter Eleven

The Book of 1 Chronicles

David Defeats His Enemies

"When the Philistines heard that David had been anointed king over all Israel, they all went up in search of David; and he heard about it and went out against them. Now the Philistines had come and made a raid in the Valley of Rephaim. So David inquired of God, "Shall I go up against the Philistines? And will You hand them over to me?" Then the LORD said to him, "Go up, and I will hand them over to you." So Israel came up to Baal-perazim, and David defeated the Philistines there. Then David said, "God has broken through my enemies by my hand, like the breakthrough of waters." Therefore they named that place Baal-perazim. The Philistines abandoned their gods (idols) there; so David gave a command and they were burned in a fire [as the Law of Moses required]. The Philistines again made a raid in the valley. So David inquired again of God, and God said to him, "Do not go up after them; circle around behind them and come at them in front of the balsam trees. It shall be when you hear the sound of marching in the tops of the balsam trees, then you shall go out to battle, for God has gone out before you to strike the Philistine army." So David did just as God had commanded him, and they struck down the army of the Philistines from Gibeon as far as Gezer. Then David's fame spread into all the lands; and the LORD caused all nations to fear him." – 1 Chronicles 14:8-17 AMP

God is very strategic. When the Philistines heard that David had been anointed king of Israel, they came to pick a fight, so we find David asking God, "Shall I go up? and will you hand them over to me?" There is nothing wrong with getting counsel from God concerning your movements or battles. He may say, "No, don't jump in this battle it has nothing to do with you," or he may say, "There is a little sheep that's about to go astray, cover them in intercession." Just ask.

God told David to go up and that He would hand them over, so they were defeated as God promised. The Philistines returned and David inquires again of God. This time God tells him, "Do not go up after them. Circle behind them and come at them from another direction."

Intercessors it may be the same enemy, but God can and will give you a different strategy to fight them. David did just what God commanded and the enemy was struck down, and David's fame spread.

When you are attacking the enemy and you defeat him, the next time you fight it won't be the same imps as before. You will fight those that are on your level, but it's fine, because you will win.

David's Prayer of Gratitude

"Then David the king went in and sat before the LORD and said, "Who am I, O LORD God, and what is my house and family that You have brought me this far? This was a small thing in Your eyes, O God; but You have spoken of Your servant's house for a great while to come, and have regarded me according to the standard and estate of a man of high degree (prominence), O LORD God. What more can David say to You for the honor granted to Your servant? For You know Your servant. O LORD, for Your servant's sake, and in accordance with Your own heart, You have accomplished all this greatness, to make known all these great things. O LORD, there is no one like You, nor is there any God except You, according to all that we have heard with our ears. And what

one nation on the earth is like Your people Israel, whom God went to redeem for Himself as a people, to make a name for Yourself by great and awesome and terrible things, by driving out nations from before Your people, whom You redeemed out of Egypt? You made Your people Israel Your own people forever, and You, LORD, became their God. "Therefore now, O LORD, let the word which You have spoken concerning Your servant and his house endure forever, and do as You have said. Let Your name [and the character that it denotes] endure and be magnified forever, saying, 'The LORD of hosts is the God of Israel, yes, a God to Israel; and the house of Your servant David is established before You.' For You, O my God, have revealed to Your servant that You will build for him a house (descendants); therefore Your servant has found courage to pray before You. And now, O LORD, You are God, and you have spoken and promised this good thing to Your servant. Therefore may it please You to bless the house (descendants) of Your servant, that it may continue before You forever; for what You bless, O LORD, is blessed forever.""

- 1 Chronicles 17:16-27 AMP

Being grateful is one key to going very far in God. Learn how to acknowledge God for everything that He does for you. Like David when you have alone time with God, remind Him of the many things that He has done and the ways that he has made on your behalf. Remind him of the promises that he has made and kept when it came to your family, friends, children and your job. Begin to let your mind go back to prophetic words that have come to pass. Think on the different times that He has healed your body, and how what other people have perished from, only made you stronger.

    David knew how to be grateful. He sat before God and allowed his mind to go back to when he was a little boy keeping his father's flocks. How far back can you go?

Do you remember when the enemy tried to make someone do harm to you but right when they thought they had you cornered God stepped in.

"Oh, give thanks to the Lord, for he is good! For His mercy endures forever." - Psalm 107:1

David's Pride and Arrogance to Count the People

Read 2 Chronicles 21:7-17. As intercessors, we have to be careful not to allow pride to come into our life and cause us to do things that will upset God. David, being motivated by pride, sent Joab to number the people. This action was David focusing on numbers and not on God. After it was done, David knew that he had made a major mistake. He repented but the damage had been done. God sends Gad, the seer the prophet, to David who tells David that God has chosen three punishments for him, but that he gets to decide which one it will be.

From this we see that there are consequences to our sins. If there is any pride, remove it or you can pray, "Lord I don't know if I have any pride in me, but if I do, please reveal it to me so that I can deal with it immediately."

David made a choice and God released a plague that killed seventy thousand people, but God had mercy and told the angel to stop where he was because he had done enough. I thank God for his mercy that endures forever.

David Builds An Altar

The angel tells Gad to tell David that he needs to build an altar to the Lord on the threshing floor of Ornan, so David purchases the threshing floor and all of the oxen, the wood and the wheat that would be needed from Ornan for six hundred shekels of gold; and he builds an altar to the Lord and presents burnt offerings and peace offerings. He calls on the Lord and God answers by accepting the offerings that he has presented to him and sending fire to consume it.

Intercessors what do you have that would be considered a suitable sacrifice to God? What can you give to him?

"I beseech[a] you therefore, brethren, by the mercies of God, that you present your bodies a living sacrifice, holy, acceptable to God, which is your [b]reasonable service." – Romans 12:1

Intercessor, present yourself to God. This is the least that we can do.

David Instructs Solomon On Having A Prayer Life

""As for you, Solomon my son, know the God of your father [have personal knowledge of Him, be acquainted with, and understand Him; appreciate, heed, and cherish Him] and serve Him with a blameless heart and a willing mind; for the LORD searches all hearts and minds, and understands every intent and inclination of the thoughts. If you seek Him [inquiring for and of Him and requiring Him as your first and vital necessity] He will let you find Him; but if you abandon (turn away from) Him, He will reject you forever. Consider this carefully, for the

LORD has chosen you to build a house for the sanctuary. Be courageous and strong and do it.""

– 1 Chronicles 28:9-10 AMP

In this passage we see David teaching Solomon concerning prayer. He laid a foundation that would follow Solomon all the days of his life. Just as David took time to instruct Solomon, you should also spend time teaching your children, grandchildren and others that you have influence over how to commune with God. Take them aside and show them what it is to pray for someone else. This is what we are to do as intercessors, train others. Little children are taught how to use phones and tablets. Teaching them how to pray is a needed investment that will pay off in the long run.

David's Prayer of Praise and Thanksgiving

"Therefore David blessed the LORD in the sight of all the assembly and said, "Blessed (praised, adored, and thanked) are You, O LORD God of Israel (Jacob) our father, forever and ever. Yours, O LORD, is the greatness and the power and the glory and the victory and the majesty, indeed everything that is in the heavens and on the earth; Yours is the dominion and kingdom, O LORD, and You exalt Yourself as head over all. Both riches and honor come from You, and You rule over all. In Your hand is power and might; and it is in Your hands to make great and to give strength to everyone. Now therefore, our God, we thank You, and praise Your glorious name. "But who am I, and who are my people, that we should be able to offer as generously as this? For all things come from You, and from Your own hand we have given to You. For we are sojourners before You, and tenants, as all our fathers were; our days on the earth are like a shadow, and there is no hope [of remaining]. O LORD our God, all this abundance that we have

prepared to build You a house for Your holy Name, it is from Your hand, and is all Your own. I know also, my God, that You test the heart and delight in uprightness and integrity. In the uprightness of my heart I have willingly offered all these things. So now with joy I have seen Your people who are present here, make their offerings willingly and freely to You. O LORD, God of Abraham, Isaac, and Israel, our fathers, keep forever such purposes and thoughts in the minds of Your people, and direct their hearts toward You; and give to my son Solomon a perfect heart to keep Your commandments, Your testimonies, and Your statutes, and to do all [that is necessary] to build the temple [for You], for which I have made provision." Then David said to all the assembly, "Now bless (praise, thank) the LORD your God." And all the assembly blessed the LORD, the God of their fathers, and bowed down and honored the LORD and to the king [as His earthly representative]."

- 1 Chronicles 29:10-20 AMP

David stood in front of the congregation and blessed God. I don't think he was ashamed. When you look at David's life and your life, shame should never be allowed to take a seat in your mind or your heart. You have some people that can talk about anything and everything, but can you thank and praise God for just being God? You can never bless God enough. Just when you think you have thanked him enough, you think of something else that He has done. You should always have a heart of gratitude. If God never does anything else, He has already done enough for you to say thank you.

"But we will bless the Lord from this time forth and forevermore." - Psalm 115:18

Chapter Twelve

The Book of 2 Chronicles

Solomon Prays for Wisdom

"That night God appeared to Solomon and said to him, "Ask what I shall give to you." Then Solomon said to God, "You have shown great lovingkindness and mercy to my father David, and have made me king in his place. Now, O LORD God, Your promise to my father David is fulfilled, for You have made me king over a people as numerous as the dust of the earth. Give me wisdom and knowledge, so that I may go out and come in [performing my duties] before this people, for [otherwise] who can rule and administer justice to this great people of Yours?" God replied to Solomon, "Because this was in your heart and you did not ask for riches, possessions or honor and personal glory, or the life of those who hate you, nor have you even asked for long life, but you have asked for wisdom and knowledge for yourself so that you may rule and administer justice to My people over whom I have made you king, wisdom and knowledge have been granted you. I will also give you riches, possessions, and honor, such as none of the kings who were before you has possessed nor will those who will come after you." So Solomon went from the high place at Gibeon, from the Tent of Meeting, to Jerusalem. And he reigned over Israel." - 2 Chronicles 1:7-13 AMP

God came to Solomon in a dream and asks him what he wants. Solomon tells God that the promise that he had made to his father David had been fulfilled through him; and that he desired wisdom to know how to govern and to perform his duties as king. God granted Solomon's request.

Intercessors, God does examine our hearts, so let's make sure that our motives are right before Him. When you ask for something from God, ask yourself if you want it just to flaunt it or if you will use it for the kingdom. Why do you desire certain gifts from Him? Is it so that you can be used for His glory or is it that you might receive glory and have all eyes on you?

Solomon's Prayer for the Temple

"Then Solomon stood before the altar of the LORD in the presence of the entire assembly of Israel and spread out his hands. For Solomon had made a bronze platform, five cubits square and three cubits high, and had set it in the midst of the courtyard; and he stood on it, and he knelt down on his knees in the presence of all the assembly of Israel and spread out his hands toward heaven, and he said, "O LORD, God of Israel, there is no god like You in heaven or on the earth, keeping covenant and showing mercy and lovingkindness to Your servants who walk before You [in obedience] with all their heart, [You] who have kept Your promise to Your servant David, my father, that which You told him; You have spoken with Your mouth and have fulfilled it with Your hand, as it is today. Now therefore, O LORD, the God of Israel, keep with Your servant David, my father, that which You promised him, saying, 'You shall not fail to have a man to sit on the throne of Israel, provided your sons are careful to walk in My law as you, [David,] have walked before Me.' Now then, O LORD, the God of Israel, let Your word which You have spoken to Your servant David be confirmed (verified). "But will God actually dwell with mankind on the earth? Behold, heaven and the highest heaven cannot contain You; how much less this house which I have built! Yet have regard for the prayer of Your servant and for his supplication, O LORD my God, to listen to the cry and to the prayer which Your servant prays before You, that Your eyes may be open toward this house day and night, toward the place in which You have said that You would put

Your Name (Presence), to listen to the prayer which Your servant shall pray toward this place. So listen to the requests of Your servant and Your people Israel when they pray toward this place. Hear from Your dwelling place, from heaven; and when You hear, forgive." – 2 Chronicles 6:12-21 AMP

The temple has been completed and Solomon, standing before the people, acknowledges that there is no God like the God of Israel who has never broken a covenant and has always kept His promises. If He said it, He will do it. Solomon tells to God that He is bigger than the universe and questions how He can fit into the temple that has been prepared for Him. He admonishes God to accept his prayers
 Intercessors, you are the temple of the living God. He lives on the inside of you; so you can make your petitions known to Him and for that you should be grateful.

Solomon's Prayers of Supplication and Intercession Continue

In 2 Chronicles 6-7, Solomon prays extensively and offers up intercession on behalf of the people of Israel. We should all intercede for others as extensively as Solomon interceded.

God Fights for Judah

"But Jeroboam had set an ambush to come from the rear, so that Israel was in front of Judah and the ambush was behind them. When [the men of] Judah turned around, they were attacked from both front and rear; so they cried out to the LORD [for help], and the priests blew the trumpets. Then the men of Judah raised a war cry; and as they shouted, God struck Jeroboam and all Israel [with defeat] before Abijah and Judah.

And the sons of Israel fled before Judah, and God handed over the sons of Israel to them. Thus the sons of Israel were subdued (humbled) at that time, and the sons of Judah prevailed because they relied on the LORD, the God of their fathers." - 2 Chronicles 13:13-18 AMP

In this passage, Judah prevailed because they relied on the Lord God of their fathers. Intercessors the battle that you are in may seem hopeless to you, and the enemy may have you surrounded and you feel that there is no way out, but when you open your mouth and cry out to God the victory will be handed to you.

Asa Instructs the People to Pray

"Asa did what was good and right in the sight of the LORD his God. He removed the foreign altars and high places and tore down the [pagan] pillars (obelisks, memorial stones), and cut to pieces the Asherim [the symbols of the goddess Asherah]. And he commanded Judah to seek the LORD God of their fathers [to inquire of and for Him and seek Him as a vital necessity], and to observe the law [given to Moses] and the commandment."
- 2 Chronicles 14:2-4 AMP

Asa did what was good and right in the sight of the Lord his God. The foreign altars, high places, and pagan pillars were removed; and the Asherim were cut to pieces and he commanded Judah to seek the Lord God of their fathers and to observe His laws. Intercessors, just like king Asa, begin removing those things that hinder you from fully seeking the Lord God and once that is done, you will be able to lead others to Him.

God Fights for Asa and Judah

"Now Zerah the Ethiopian (Cushite) came out against Judah with an army of a million men and three hundred chariots, and he came as far as Mareshah. Then Asa went out against him, and they drew up in battle formation in the Valley of Zephathah at Mareshah. Asa called out to the LORD his God, saying, "O LORD, there is no one besides You to help in the battle between the powerful and the weak; so help us, O LORD our God, for we trust in and rely on You, and in Your name we have come against this multitude. O LORD, You are our God; let not man prevail against You." So the LORD struck the Ethiopians [with defeat] before Asa and Judah, and the Ethiopians fled. Asa and the people who were with him pursued them as far as Gerar; and so many Ethiopians fell that none of them were found alive; for they were destroyed before the LORD and His army. And they carried away a very large amount of spoil. They attacked and destroyed all the cities around Gerar, for the dread of the LORD had fallen on them. They plundered all the cities, for there was a large amount of spoil in them. They also struck down the people [living] in tents who had livestock, and took captive large numbers of sheep and camels. Then they returned to Jerusalem."
- 2 Chronicles 14:9-15 AMP

Just as God was with Asa and gave him victory, God and His army are with you and will give you victory. Be prepared to walk away with great spoils!

Changes Made By Asa

"They entered into a covenant (solemn agreement) to seek the LORD God of their fathers with all their heart and soul; and that whoever would not seek the LORD God of Israel, was to be put to death, whether young or old, man or woman. They swore an oath to the LORD with a loud voice, with [jubilant] shouting, with trumpets, and with horns. All Judah rejoiced over the oath, for they had sworn with all their heart and had sought Him with their whole heart, and He let them find Him. So the LORD gave them rest on every side."

- 2 Chronicles 15:12-15 AMP

Asa and the people entered into a covenant with God. Intercessors, have you entered into a covenant to seek after God with your whole heart or are you satisfied with staying on the surface?

God Helps Jehosophat

"So [Ahab] the king of Israel and Jehoshaphat king of Judah went up against Ramoth-gilead. The king of Israel said to Jehoshaphat, "I will disguise myself and will go into battle, but you put on your [royal] robes." So the king of Israel disguised himself, and they went into the battle. Now the king of Aram (Syria) had commanded the captains of his chariots, saying, "Do not fight with the small or the great, but only with the king of Israel." So when the captains of the chariots saw Jehoshaphat [of Judah], they said, "It is the king of Israel!" So they turned to fight against him, but Jehoshaphat called out [for God's help], and the LORD helped him; and God diverted them away from him." - 2 Chronicles 18:28-31 AMP

Just as Jehosophat almost lost his life because of who he was attached to, it is important that we be mindful of who we attach ourselves to. Going into battle with the wrong person could cost you your life and your soul.

Jehosophat Calls A Fast

"Now it happened after this that the Moabites and the Ammonites, together with some of the Meunites, came to make war against Jehoshaphat. Then it was reported to Jehoshaphat, "A great multitude has come against you from beyond the [Dead] Sea, out of Aram (Syria); and behold, they are in Hazazon-tamar (that is, Engedi)." Then Jehoshaphat was afraid and set himself [determinedly, as his vital need] to seek the LORD; and he proclaimed a fast throughout all Judah. So [the people of] Judah gathered together to seek help from the LORD; indeed they came from all the cities of Judah to seek the LORD [longing for Him with all their heart]."
- 2 Chronicles 20:1-4 AMP

Upon hearing about the mobilization of the Moabites and the Ammonites, King Jehoshaphat fears what is to come, so he seeks the Lord for help and calls a fast.
    Intercessors when you get news that may cause you to lose hope in God there is nothing wrong with fasting. Jehoshaphat stands before the people with all eyes on him and he begins to cry out to the Lord, "Are you not in heaven? Are you not in control?" As he continues to remind God of what He said He would do in regards to their enemies, he prays and says, "God we are powerless against this great multitude that is heading towards us. We don't know what to do, but our eyes are on you?"

Intercession Is Made By Jehosophat

"Then Jehoshaphat stood in the assembly of Judah and Jerusalem, in the house of the LORD in front of the new

courtyard, and said, "O LORD, God of our fathers, are You not God in heaven? And do You not rule over all the kingdoms of the nations? Power and might are in Your hand, there is no one able to take a stand against You. O our God, did You not drive out the inhabitants of this land before Your people Israel and give it forever to the descendants of Your friend Abraham? They have lived in it, and have built You a sanctuary in it for Your Name, saying, 'If evil comes on us, or the sword of judgment, or plague, or famine, we will stand before this house and before You (for Your Name and Your Presence is in this house) and we will cry out to You in our distress, and You will hear and save us.' Now behold, the sons of Ammon and Moab and Mount Seir, whom You would not allow Israel to invade when they came from the land of Egypt (for they turned away from them and did not destroy them), here they are, rewarding us by coming to drive us out of Your possession which You have given us as an inheritance. O our God, will You not judge them? For we are powerless against this great multitude which is coming against us. We do not know what to do, but our eyes are on You." So all Judah stood before the LORD, with their infants, their wives, and their children."

- 2 Chronicles 20:5-13 AMP

Intercessors, whenever you feel powerless in a situation, just listen. While you are waiting, just listen. Don't be so eager to move from where you are. Just listen, the answer that you need is forthcoming.

The Answer to Prayer Is Given

"Then in the midst of the assembly the Spirit of the LORD came upon Jahaziel the son of Zechariah, the son of Benaiah, the son of Jeiel, the son of Mattaniah, a Levite of the sons of Asaph. He said, "Listen carefully, all [you people of] Judah, and you inhabitants of Jerusalem, and King Jehoshaphat. The

LORD says this to you: 'Be not afraid or dismayed at this great multitude, for the battle is not yours, but God's. ~'Go down against them tomorrow. Behold, they will come up by the ascent of Ziz, and you will find them at the end of the river valley, in front of the Wilderness of Jeruel. ~'You need not fight in this battle; take your positions, stand and witness the salvation of the LORD who is with you, O Judah and Jerusalem. Do not fear or be dismayed; tomorrow go out against them, for the LORD is with you.'" Jehoshaphat bowed with his face to the ground, and all Judah and the inhabitants of Jerusalem fell down before the LORD, worshiping Him. The Levites, from the sons of the Kohathites and the sons of the Korahites, stood up to praise the LORD God of Israel, with a very loud voice." - 2 Chronicles 20:14-19 AMP

While the people were waiting for an answer from the Lord concerning what they should do, the spirit of the Lord moved upon Jahaziel, a Levite, one of the sons of Asaph and he said, "Everybody listen very carefully. The Lord says do not be afraid of the people that are coming this way. The battle is not yours but God's." As an intercessor there are some battles that you feel that you just can't win, but know this one thing, your God fights for you and you will have no need to fight like the children of Israel. All God wants you to do is to take your position and stand, don't fear the unknown because God is with you and He will fight for you.

After receiving what they needed from the Lord the people fell down before the Lord worshiping him. Don't forget to worship him while you're waiting on Him to do what He has promised He would do.

"Make a joyful noise to the Lord, all you lands! Serve the Lord with gladness! Come before His presence with singing! Know (perceive, recognize, and understand with approval) that the

Lord is God! It is He Who has made us, not we ourselves [and we are His]! We are His people and the sheep of His pasture. [Eph. 2:10.] Enter into His gates with thanksgiving and a thank offering and into His courts with praise! Be thankful and say so to Him, bless and affectionately praise His name! For the Lord is good; His mercy and loving-kindness are everlasting, His faithfulness and truth endure to all generations."

- Psalm 100:1-5 AMP

Uzziah Made King

"Uzziah was sixteen years old when he became king, and he reigned fifty-two years in Jerusalem. His mother's name was Jechiliah of Jerusalem. He did right in the sight of the LORD, in accordance with everything that his father Amaziah had done. He continued to seek God in the days of Zechariah, who had understanding through the vision of God; and as long as he sought (inquired of, longing for) the LORD, God caused him to prosper." – 2 Chronicles 26:3-5 AMP

We must learn to be consistent in our walk with God as well as our prayer life. Don't fall off when you are tested; and don't give up on God. When you don't know what the outcome of a thing will be, that is the best time to strengthen your resolve, and dig in and push through. God wants to prosper you, but you must maintain your drive and go forward. Don't leave your post, stay on the wall your prayers are needed.

Hezekiah Prays for the Ceremonially Unclean

"For the majority of the people, many from Ephraim and Manasseh, Issachar and Zebulun, had not purified themselves, and yet they ate the Passover contrary to what had been prescribed. For Hezekiah had prayed for them, saying, "May the good LORD pardon everyone who sets his heart to seek God--the LORD God of his fathers--even though it is not in accordance with the [ceremonial] purification [rules] of the sanctuary." So the LORD listened to Hezekiah and healed the people [of their uncleanness]." – 2 Chronicles 30:18-20 AMP

What an awesome example Hezekiah has provided for us in the Word of God. Four of the twelve tribes had not prepared themselves in order to eat of the Passover Feast, so Hezekiah not wanting anyone to feel left out, prays for those who were termed ceremonially unclean and asks the Lord to pardon everyone who had set there heart to seek God. The Lord listened and healed the people of their uncleanliness.

Intercessors you can do it too. Pray and ask God to forgive and heal.

" If you forgive the sins of any, they are forgiven them; if you retain the sins of any, they are retained." – John 20:23 NKJV

The Priests and the Levites Pray A Blessing Over the People

"Then the whole assembly decided to celebrate [the feast] for another seven days; and they celebrated it another seven days with joy. For Hezekiah king of Judah gave to the assembly 1,000 bulls and 7,000 sheep, and the officials gave the assembly 1,000 bulls and 10,000 sheep. And a large number of priests consecrated themselves [for service]. All the assembly of Judah rejoiced, with the priests and the Levites and all the assembly that came from Israel, both the sojourners (resident aliens, foreigners) who came from the land of Israel and those living in Judah. So there was great joy in Jerusalem, because there had been nothing like this in Jerusalem since the time of Solomon the son of David, king of Israel. Then the priests and

Levites stood and blessed the people; and their voice was heard and their prayer came up to His holy dwelling place, to heaven." - 2 Chronicles 30:23-27 AMP

In this passage the king of Assyria has come to Judah in order to invade the city, so while the Assyrians are camped on the outskirts of Judah, King Hezekiah begins making preparations on the inside of the city in case a long siege lies in front of them.

Intercessors, you may not know how long the battle may be that you will have to engage in, but make preparations for your city with fasting and more prayer. Stay prayed up and strengthen yourself because your siege may be for longer than you anticipate. Also, encourage one another in the Lord. This is what Hezekiah did. He gave people a morale booster, so go and boost someone's morale. Encourage them, pray over them and bless them. The enemy likes to boast about his exploits, about how many kills he has, and about the territory that he has taken. If that doesn't work, then he wants to speak badly about your leadership. Isn't that just like the devil to toot his own horn, while making someone else look inferior? Hear me good intercessors, don't believe the lies of the devil. Don't be moved even when the enemy brings railing accusations against your God. I promise you that the God that you serve has something that the devil won't see coming. As you continue to cry out like Hezekiah and the prophet Isaiah in prayer to the Lord, He will send an angel to cut down every adversary that tried to withstand you and He will deliver you.

Hezekiah's Prayer Is Answered Again

In 2 Chronicles 32:1-20, we see Hezekiah praying, and God responding by destroying the Assyrian army. In 2 Chronicles 32:24-26, we see him praying once again, but this time for his own health.

"In those days Hezekiah became terminally ill; and he prayed to the LORD, and He answered him and gave him a [miraculous] sign. But Hezekiah did nothing [for the LORD] in return for the benefit bestowed on him, because his heart had become proud; therefore God's wrath came on him and on Judah and Jerusalem. However, Hezekiah humbled his proud heart, both he and the inhabitants of Jerusalem, so that the wrath of the LORD did not come on them during the days of Hezekiah." - 2 Chronicles 32:24-26 AMP

As intercessors it is important that we learn to function with a gracious heart, and not function in pride and act as if God owes us something because in reality he owes us nothing. Should you become sick, and God heals you, Lord I thank you, is the right response. Not, 'Well what took you so long? You should have done it before now." Examine your heart and repent. Ask to be forgiven for all of your ungodly behavior.

"Repent therefore of this your wickedness, and pray God if perhaps the thought of your heart may be forgiven you."
– Acts 8:22 NKJV

God Answers Manasseh's Prayer

"Now the LORD spoke to Manasseh and to his people, but they paid no attention. So the LORD brought the commanders of the army of the king of Assyria against them, and they

captured Manasseh with hooks [through his nose or cheeks] and bound him with bronze [chains] and took him to Babylon. But when he was in distress, he sought the LORD his God and humbled himself greatly before the God of his fathers. When he prayed to Him, He was moved by his entreaty and heard his pleading, and brought him back to Jerusalem to his kingdom. Then Manasseh knew that the LORD is God."
- 2 Chronicles 33:10-13 AMP

As intercessors, we have to have a humble heart. We cannot be puffed up with pride. There is nothing good about pride; and we cannot pray effectively when we have issues with it. Get rid of pride or it will eventually be the ruin of you.

"When pride comes, then comes shame; But with the humble is wisdom." - Proverbs 11:2 NKJV

"And whoever exalts himself will be humbled, and he who humbles himself will be exalted."- Matthew 23:12 NKJV

Josiah Seeks God

"Josiah was eight years old when he became king, and he reigned for thirty-one years in Jerusalem. He did what was right in the sight of the LORD, and walked in the ways of David his father (forefather) and did not turn aside either to the right or to the left. For in the eighth year of his reign, while he was still young (sixteen), he began to seek after and inquire of the God of his father David; and in the twelfth year he began to purge Judah and Jerusalem of the high places, the Asherim, and the carved and cast images." - 2 Chronicles 34:1-3 AMP

Josiah was eight years old he became king, and while he was young he had advisors that oversaw his life and instructed him in the things of the Lord including how to seek the face of God, how to inquire of Him, and how to acknowledge the Lord God in all of His ways so that God could direct his path.

Intercessors you may have children and grandchildren who need your counsel and your wisdom. Guide them into the path that God has directed for them to go. Their parents may not believe like you do, but whenever they come to your home or are around you, impart into them. Don't allow them to leave empty. You have plenty of oil on reserve, so pour out and train them up.

"Train up a child in the way he should go, And when he is old he will not depart from it." – Proverbs 22:6 NKJV

Chapter Thirteen

The Book of Ezra

A Prayer of Blessing

"Blessed be the LORD, the God of our fathers [said Ezra], who put such a thing as this in the king's heart, to adorn and glorify the house of the LORD in Jerusalem, and has extended His mercy and lovingkindness to me before the king, his advisers, and all the king's mighty officials. I was strengthened and encouraged, for the hand of the LORD my God was upon me, and I gathered together outstanding men of Israel to go up with me [to Jerusalem]." - Ezra 7:27-28 AMP

In this passage, Ezra blesses the Lord God and gives him honor because he knew it was the Lord who had touched the king's heart to give him a letter. This letter provided for the needs of the house of God, which included an abundance of silver and gold, instructions on how it was to be spent, and bulls, rams and lambs, and all the other items that would be needed for a grain and drink offering.

Intercessors, when God gives you an assignment to fulfill, he always makes provision and gives you far more than you could ever have imagined.

"The blessing of the Lord makes one rich, And He adds no sorrow with it." – Proverbs 10:22 NKJV

Fasting and Prayer for God's Protection

"Then I proclaimed a fast there at the river Ahava, so that we might humble ourselves before our God to seek from Him a safe journey for us, our children, and all our possessions. For I was ashamed to request troops and horsemen from the king to protect us from the enemy along the way, because we had told the king, "The hand of our God is favorable toward all those who seek Him, but His power and His anger are against all those who abandon (turn away from) Him." So we fasted and sought [help from] our God concerning this [matter], and He heard our plea." - Ezra 8:21-23 AMP

As Ezra did, sometimes a fast coupled with prayer is needed to help maintain a clear objective, especially when you are a shepherd over a people like Ezra. Ezra had many men, women and children traveling with him to Jerusalem, so fasting and praying for God's protection was necessary. He couldn't just think about himself. Intercessors, there is no need to feel ashamed because the hand of God is on you because you are seeking His will and His ways. Follow through with your assignment, and as you fast and pray God will answer.

"I love those who love me, And those who seek me diligently will find me." – Proverbs 8:17 NKJV

Reconciling Themselves Back to God

"Now while Ezra was praying and confessing, weeping and laying himself face down before the house of God, a very large group from Israel, of men, women, and children, gathered to him, for the people wept bitterly. Shecaniah the son of Jehiel, of the sons of Elam, said to Ezra, "We have been unfaithful to our God and have married foreign women from the peoples of the

land; yet now there is hope for Israel in spite of this. Therefore let us now make a covenant with our God to send away all the [foreign] wives and their children, in accordance with the advice of my lord and of those who tremble [in reverent obedience] at the commandment of our God; and let it be done in accordance with the Law. Stand up, for it is your duty, and we will be with you. Be brave and act." Then Ezra stood and made the leaders of the priests, the Levites, and all Israel, take an oath that they would act in accordance with this proposal; so they took the oath. Then Ezra got up from before the house of God and went into the chamber of Jehohanan the son of Eliashib [and spent the night there]. He did not eat bread nor drink water, for he was mourning over the [former] exiles' faithlessness." - Ezra 10:1-6 AMP

The peoples' unfaithfulness to God has sent Ezra into a place of lamenting before God. The things that God had clearly told them not to do, they had done that and more. Even some of the Levites and leaders, were disobedient, marrying foreign wives, and through these marriages, conceiving children.

Intercessors, it happens. You can counsel women and men, and tell them what they should or shouldn't do, but if they are not rooted and grounded in God, the flesh will go after what it wants, and once it gets what it wants there is no satisfaction to be had.

The people eventually came to Ezra and acknowledged that they had been unfaithful to God and had married people that they shouldn't have, but they were willing to send make a covenant and send those men and women away.

As an intercessor, you may have to counsel those you know went against the will of God and did it their way, but I guarantee you this, God will direct you on how to handle the matter.

Chapter Fourteen

The Book of Nehemiah

Nehemiah Travails In Prayer

"And they said to me, The remnant there in the province who escaped exile are in great trouble and reproach; the wall of Jerusalem is broken down, and its [fortified] gates are destroyed by fire. When I heard this, I sat down and wept and mourned for days and fasted and prayed [constantly] before the God of heaven, And I said, O Lord God of heaven, the great and terrible God, Who keeps covenant, loving-kindness, and mercy for those who love Him and keep His commandments, Let Your ear now be attentive and Your eyes open to listen to the prayer of Your servant which I pray before You day and night for the Israelites, Your servants, confessing the sins of the Israelites which we have sinned against You. Yes, I and my father's house have sinned. We have acted very corruptly against You and have not kept the commandments, statutes, and ordinances which You commanded Your servant Moses. [Deut. 6:1-9.] Remember [earnestly] what You commanded Your servant Moses: If you transgress and are unfaithful, I will scatter you abroad among the nations; [Lev. 26:33.] But if you return to Me and keep My commandments and do them, though your outcasts were in the farthest part of the heavens [the expanse of outer space], yet will I gather them from there and will bring them to the place in which I have chosen to set My Name. [Deut. 30:1-5.] Now these are Your servants and Your people, whom You have redeemed by Your great power and by Your strong hand. O Lord, let Your ear be attentive to the prayer of Your servant and the prayer of Your servants who delight to

revere and fear Your name (Your nature and attributes); and prosper, I pray You, Your servant this day and grant him mercy in the sight of this man. For I was cupbearer to the king." - Nehemiah 1:3-11 AMPC

News had gotten back to Nehemiah concerning the escaped exiles that were in trouble, and he was saddened to hear that the wall in Jerusalem was in disrepair and that the gates burned with fire. This news caused him to weep and mourn, so he fasted and interceded, and began to confess the sins of everyone, including himself. He acknowledged their wrongdoing and repented.

Intercessors, we should always do a heart check just in case we may have thought something, said something, or done something outside of the will of God. Ultimately, it's important that our heart is right before God, so that He can hear and receive our prayers.

"For all have sinned and fall short of the glory of God."
- Romans 3:23 NKJV

The Prayers of Nehemiah Are Heard and Answered

"So the king said to me, "Why do you look sad when you are not sick? This is nothing but sadness of heart." Then I was very frightened, and I said to the king, "Let the king live forever. Why should my face not be sad when the city, the place of my fathers' tombs, lies desolate and its gates have been consumed by fire?" The king said to me, "What do you request?" So I prayed to the God of heaven. I said to the king, "If it pleases the king, and if your servant has found favor in your presence, [I ask] that you send me to Judah, to the city of my fathers' tombs, so that I may rebuild it." The king, beside whom the queen was sitting, asked me, "How long will your journey take, and when will you return?" So it pleased the king to send me,

and I gave him a definite time [for my return]. Then I said to the king, "If it pleases the king, let letters be given to me for the governors of the provinces beyond the [Euphrates] River, so that they will allow me to pass through until I reach Judah, and a letter to Asaph, the keeper of the king's forest, so that he will give me timber to construct beams for the gates of the fortress which is by the temple, and for the city wall and for the house which I will occupy." And the king granted me what I asked, for the good hand of my God was upon me."
- Nehemiah 2:2-8 AMP

God begins to move on the intercession of Nehemiah. Nehemiah desired to return to Judah to help with the repairs, and the opportunity presented itself as he stood before the king.

God will make provision for you to carry out the assignment that He has placed on your hearts. At first glance it may have seemed like a negative response was coming, but look at God, He turned it around for Nehemiah's good and he was able to leave his position as cupbearer to the king and go to Judah for a set amount of time. Nehemiah needed favor and God gave him favor.

Like Nehemiah, God will give you the favor needed to get the job done. So when the time presents itself, God will put what you need to say into your mouth. The way has already been made.

" I am the Lord your God, Who brought you out of the land of Egypt; Open your mouth wide, and I will fill it."
- Psalm 81: 10 NKJV

The Work of Rebuilding Is Ridiculed

"But when Sanballat heard that we were rebuilding the wall, he became furious, completely enraged, and he ridiculed the

Jews. He spoke before his brothers and the army of Samaria, "What are these feeble Jews doing? Can they restore it for themselves? Can they offer sacrifices? Can they finish in a day? Can they revive the stones from the heaps of dust and rubbish, even the ones that have been burned?" Now Tobiah the Ammonite was beside him, and he said, "Even what they are building--if a fox should get up on it, he would break down their stone wall." [And Nehemiah prayed] Hear, O our God, how we are despised! Return their taunts on their own heads. Give them up as prey in a land of captivity. Do not forgive their wrongdoing and do not let their sin be wiped out before You, for they have offended the builders [and provoked You]."
- Nehemiah 4:1-5 AMP

The enemy may press upon you like he did Nehemiah and those who were working along with him to do the needed repairs on the wall, but Nehemiah prayed prophetically and said, "Lord we are despised, but the things that have been spoken over us, we return back to the sender. We don't believe their report. Our trust is in you and you alone, so don't allow them to get away unscathed and don't blot out their sin from before you for they have offended us and you." Like Nehemiah, when the enemy presses in, presses in to God, and pray.

"Death and life are in the power of the tongue, And those who love it will eat its fruit." - Proverbs 18:21 NKJV

The Spirit of Discouragement is Overcome By Prayer

"So we built the wall and the entire wall was joined together to half its height, for the people had a heart to work. But when Sanballat, Tobiah, the Arabs, the Ammonites, and the Ashdodites heard that the repair of the walls of Jerusalem went on, and that the breaches were being closed, they were very

angry. They all conspired together to come and to fight against Jerusalem, and to cause a disturbance in it. But we prayed to our God, and because of them we set up a guard against them day and night. Then [the leaders of] Judah said, "The strength of the burden bearers is failing, And there is much rubble; We ourselves are unable To rebuild the wall." Our enemies said, "They will not know or see us until we are among them, kill them and put a stop to the work." When the Jews who lived near them came, they said to us ten times (repeatedly), "From every place you turn, they will come up against us." So I stationed armed men behind the wall in the lowest places, at the open positions [where it was least protected]; and I stationed the people in families with their swords, spears, and bows. When I saw their fear, I stood and said to the nobles and officials and the rest of the people: "Do not be afraid of them; [confidently] remember the Lord who is great and awesome, and [with courage from Him] fight for your brothers, your sons, your daughters, your wives, and for your homes." Now when our enemies heard that we knew about their plot against us, and that God had frustrated their plan, we all returned to the wall, each one to his work." - Nehemiah 4:6-15 AMP

As you are working like Nehemiah and your work is progressing, God will give you strategies on how to out maneuver your adversary. As he comes to bring fear and discouragement in your ranks, just remember to pray. Don't forget to seek God's counsel. Even when you know your enemy is plotting to do you harm, pray. Intercessors, when fear is evident on the faces of those closest to you, encourage them to remember that the God you serve is great and mighty, and take courage and fight for those who can't fight for themselves. So when the time comes and your enemies find out that you know what they are planning and that it was God who revealed it to you and you are able to complete your assignment, give God all the glory for the things that He has done.

" Lest Satan should take advantage of us: for we are not ignorant of his devices." – 2 Corinthians 2:11 NKJV

The Plot of Sanballat

"Then Sanballat sent his servant to me in the same way the fifth time, with an open letter in his hand. In it was written, "It is reported among the [neighboring] nations, and Gashmu is saying that you and the Jews are planning to revolt, and that is the reason you are rebuilding the wall. And according to these reports, you are to be their king. Also [it is reported that] you have appointed prophets to make a proclamation concerning you in Jerusalem, saying, 'There is a king in Judah!' And now these things will be reported to the [Persian] king. So come now, and let us consult together." I sent a message to him, saying, "Such things as you are saying have not been done; you are inventing them in your own mind." For they all wanted to frighten us, thinking, "They will become discouraged with the work and it will not be done." But now, [O God,] strengthen my hands." - Nehemiah 6:5-9 AMP

People will let the devil use them to deter you from your God given mandate and assignment, but don't stop and never give up. It's just a ploy by the devil. The first time he may use intimidation, the second may be fear, the third may be a threat of bodily harm, and the fourth may be an attempt to assassinate your character, but whatever tactics the devil uses, stay the course and STAY IN YOUR LANE.

Nehemiah Asks God to Remember

"When I went into the house of Shemaiah the son of Delaiah, the son of Mehetabel, who was confined at home, he said, "Let us meet [and take refuge] together in the house of God, within the temple, and let us shut the doors of the temple, because they are coming to kill you, and they are coming to kill you at night." But I said, "Should a man like me flee [in fear and hide]? Should someone like me enter the temple [for sanctuary] to save his life? I will not go." Then I realized that God had not sent him, but he spoke this prophecy against me because Tobiah and Sanballat had hired him. He was hired for this reason, that I would be frightened and do as he said and sin, so that they would have [grounds to make] a malicious report in order to censure and disgrace me. Remember, O My God, Tobiah and Sanballat in regard to these actions of theirs, and also [remember] the prophetess Noadiah and the rest of the prophets who were trying to frighten me."
- Nehemiah 6:10-14 AMP

As Nehemiah learns in this passage, there are prophets for hire that have sold themselves to the highest bidder, and their assignment is to cause you to walk out of the perfect and divine will of God. Don't be fooled by their words. God has not sent them. They have been sent by your adversary to cause you to walk in fear and to sin and to do the very opposite of what God has told you to do.

"Certainly not! Indeed, let God be true but every man a liar. As it is written: "That you may be justified in Your words, And may overcome when You are judged." – Romans 3:4 NKJV

Ezra Offers A Prayer of Blessing

"Ezra the scribe stood on a [large] wooden platform which they had constructed for this purpose. And beside him [on the platform] stood Mattithiah, Shema, Anaiah, Uriah, Hilkiah, and Maaseiah on his right; and Pedaiah, Mishael, Malchijah, Hashum, Hashbaddanah, Zechariah, and Meshullam on his left. Ezra opened the book in the sight of all the people, for he was standing above them; and when he opened it, all the people stood up. Then Ezra blessed the LORD, the great God. And all the people answered, "Amen, Amen!" while lifting up their hands; and they knelt down and worshiped the LORD with their faces toward the ground. Also Jeshua, Bani, Sherebiah, Jamin, Akkub, Shabbethai, Hodiah, Maaseiah, Kelita, Azariah, Jozabad, Hanan, Pelaiah, and the Levites, explained the Law to the people, and the people remained in their places. So they read from the Book of the Law of God, translating and explaining it so that the people understood the reading."
- Nehemiah 8:4-8 AMP

Always remember to bless the Lord God. Never forget all that He has done for you. Tell of His goodness, and tell of His mighty acts so that those who are listening can receive strength from your testimony.

"I will bless the Lord at all times; His praise shall continually be in my mouth." - Psalm 34:1 NKJV

Confession of Sins Are Made

"Now on the twenty-fourth day of this month the Israelites assembled with fasting and in sackcloth and with dirt on their heads. The descendants of Israel (Jacob) separated themselves from all foreigners, and stood and confessed their sins and the wrongdoings of their fathers. While they stood in their places,

they read from the Book of the Law of the LORD their God for a fourth of the day and for another fourth [of it] they confessed [their sins] and worshiped the LORD their God. On the platform of the Levites stood Jeshua, Bani, Kadmiel, Shebaniah, Bunni, Sherebiah, Bani, and Chenani, and they called out with a loud voice to the LORD their God."
- Nehemiah 9:1-4 AMP

Intercessors, as I'm sure that you very well know, there is a process to cleaning up your life. Do a daily heart check and remember that confession of your sins and repenting of them will help you to stay one step ahead of your adversary who is an accuser of the brethren.

" *Confess your trespasses to one another, and pray for one another, that you may be healed. The effective, fervent prayer of a righteous man avails much."* – James 5:16 NKJV

Prayers of Praise and Worship Are Offered to the Lord

Read Nehemiah 9: 5-26. From this passage, we can see the importance of praise and worship. Wherever you are, make God's deeds known. Make them known to those who may not know that He spoke the world into existence or that He sent His son as a ransom for all. Don't be ashamed to tell of who He is to you, magnify and glorify Him for who He is and make known unto all who will listen the things that God has done. There is someone that needs to know that He is a deliverer. Someone else may need to know that He is a provider, and someone may need you to tell them that by His stripes they can be healed. Tell it intercessor! There are people that are assigned to you, and they are waiting for you to share about your God!

Reminding God of His Lovingkindness

""Therefore You handed them over to their enemies who oppressed them. But when they cried out to You in the time of their suffering and distress, You heard them from heaven, and according to Your great compassion You gave them people to rescue them. Who rescued them from the hand of their enemies. "But as soon as they had rest, they again did evil before You; Therefore You abandoned them into the hand of their enemies, so that they ruled over them. Yet when they turned and cried out again to You, You heard them from heaven, And You rescued them many times in accordance with Your compassion, And You admonished them and warned them to turn them back to Your law. Yet they acted presumptuously and arrogantly and did not heed Your commandments, but sinned against Your ordinances, Which by keeping, a man will live. But they turned a stubborn shoulder, stiffened their neck, and would not listen. "Yet You were patient with them for many years, And admonished them and warned them by Your Spirit through Your prophets; Still they would not listen. Therefore You gave them into the hand (power) of the peoples of the lands. "Yet in Your great compassion You did not utterly destroy them or abandon them, For You are a gracious and merciful God. "Now therefore, our God, the great, the mighty, and the awesome God, who keeps the covenant and lovingkindness, Do not let all the hardship seem insignificant before You, Which has come upon us, our kings, our princes, our priests, our prophets, our fathers and on all Your people, Since the time of the kings of Assyria to this day. "However, You are just and righteous in everything that has come upon us; For You have dealt faithfully, but we have acted wickedly. Our kings, our princes, our priests, and our fathers have not kept Your law Or paid attention to Your commandments and Your warnings which You have given them."

- Nehemiah 9:27-34 AMP

As Nehemiah begins to rehearse in the hearing of the people about the loving kindness of the Lord, he wants them to remember that throughout their history God has always been faithful, even when they were not. Intercessors, let's remind ourselves on a daily basis that God has always been faithful to us. Because of his tender mercies we rise to see the dawning of a new day.

"Through the Lord's mercies we are not consumed, Because His compassions fail not." – Lamentations 3:22 NKJV

Nehemiah Cleans And Purifies Everything

"Thus I cleansed and purified them from everything foreign (pagan), and I defined the duties of the priests and Levites, each one in his task; and I provided for the wood offering at appointed times and for the first fruits. O my God, [please] remember me for good [and imprint me on Your heart]."
- Nehemiah 13:30-31 AMP

When you are following the Lord's leading and He sends you to assist with the clearing away of things that had at one time caused your fellow brother or sister to stumble and fall, once the obstacles are removed out of their way, teach them how to maintain their newly gained deliverance and help to strengthen them along the way. After this is done, there is nothing wrong with asking the Lord to remember what you have done and to bless you for it.

Chapter Fifteen

The Book of Esther

Mordecai and the People Travail and Lament

"Now when Mordecai learned of everything that had been done, he tore his clothes [in mourning], and put on sackcloth and ashes, and went out into the center of the city and cried out loudly and bitterly. He went [only] as far as the king's gate, because no one was to enter the king's gate dressed in sackcloth. In each and every province that the decree and law of the king reached, there was great mourning among the Jews, with fasting, weeping and wailing; and many lay on sackcloth and ashes." - Esther 4:1-3 AMP

As Mordecai, the uncle of Queen Esther, and those who lived in nearby provinces received news of the plot of the wicked Haman to totally annihilate the Jews, Mordecai tore his clothes in mourning and all the people with one accord wept bitterly and lifted their voices as one man travailing and lamenting concerning the great loss of life that was surely to come if God did not intervene. Intercessors, when God allows dire news to reach your ears and the enemy at that very moment wants you to feel that God could not possibly deliver, know that yes God can. He is the God that can make ways out of no way. He's the same God who is ever present to meet all of your needs. So like Mordecai, if travailing prayers are needed, then by all means travail. If lamentation, then by all means lament. Use whatever God gives you to deal with that test.

Esther Intercedes

"Then Esther told them to reply to Mordecai, "Go, gather all the Jews that are present in Susa, and observe a fast for me; do not eat or drink for three days, night or day. I and my maids also will fast in the same way. Then I will go in to [see] the king [without being summoned], which is against the law; and if I perish, I perish." So Mordecai went away and did exactly as Esther had commanded him." - Esther 4:15-17 AMP

Though prayer and God are not mentioned in this text, with fasting we do realize that the two work hand in hand and are seamlessly connected. When you feel like the test that you are in is an unmovable obstacle that has come to block your progress and to keep you from going forward, then like Queen Esther find those that you know have like minded faith and ask them to fast and pray with you until God sends you the deliverance that is necessary to move your adversary out of the way. Everyone that Esther asked to fast and pray with her was on board because they all had something to lose. Their very lives were in jeopardy. The combination of prayer and fasting gives you strength and boldness to face the very thing that comes to impede your progress.

"Is this not the fast that I have chosen: To loose the bonds of wickedness, To undo the heavy burdens, To let the oppressed go free, And that you break every yoke? – Isaiah 58: 6 NKJV

Chapter Sixteen

The Book of Job

Job Worships and Blesses God Even In Adversity

"Then Job got up and tore his robe and shaved his head [in mourning for the children], and he fell to the ground and worshiped [God]. He said, "Naked (without possessions) I came [into this world] from my mother's womb, And naked I will return there. The LORD gave and the LORD has taken away; Blessed be the name of the LORD." Through all this Job did not sin nor did he blame God." - Job 1:20-22 AMP

Like Job, can you bless and honor the Lord even when calamity comes knocking at your door? Will God continue to be your mighty God? Will God still be more than enough for you? Is God still Jehovah Shammah, the light who is always present? Is he still Jehovah Shalom, your peace or will you allow bitterness and hatred towards God to overshadow your heart and to rob you of who you know Him to be?

" I will bless the Lord at all times; His praise shall continually be in my mouth. My soul shall make its boast in the Lord; The humble shall hear of it and be glad. Oh, magnify the Lord with me, And let us exalt His name together." – Psalm 34:1-3

Job Reasons With God

""What is man that You [should] magnify him [and think him important]? And that You are concerned about him? "And that

You examine him every morning And try and test him every moment? "Will You never turn Your gaze away from me [it plagues me], Nor let me alone until I swallow my spittle? "If I have sinned, what [harm] have I done to You, O Watcher of mankind? Why have You set me as a target for You, So that I am a burden to myself? "Why then do You not pardon my transgression And take away my sin and guilt? For now I will lie down in the dust; And You will seek me [diligently], but I will not be."" - Job 7:17-21 AMP

Like Job, often times we want to know why. We pray, " Lord please tell me why? What have I done so bad that has caused this thing to come on me? What did I do God? What did my children do God? Do you hate me that much? It looks like I have been singled out by you God, to be picked on, so whatever I have done forgive me and move on." With all that Job faced, he felt justified in how he addressed the situation, but before you judge Job too harshly, put yourself in his place. Wear his shoes for a while and compare his responses to yours.

Job's Despair
Read Job 10:1-22. Like Job in this passage you may have friends like Eliphaz, Bildad and Zophar who were supposedly coming to bring comfort, but by the time they were finished, that did nothing but make you feel far worse than you felt before they showed up. The entire situation that Job is dealing with has caused him to become bitter.

When God allows afflictions to come on us, he does it for a reason. The reason may not be clear to you at that very moment, but you will know in due time. Intercessors, be very careful and watchful that you don't allow bitterness to vex your spirit and take root.

" This poor man cried out, and the Lord heard him, And saved him out of all his troubles." - Psalm 34:6 NKJV

Like Job we often want the testing to end. We want God to tell us where we have gone wrong or where we have walked in error. We want an opportunity to speak so that we can ask him why we have become his enemy? But the truth is, God is never our enemy, even when we are going hardship. Every test we endure is apart of God's plan and He is there with us the entire time, we only need to reach to Him and seek His face.

" The righteous cry out, and the Lord hears, And delivers them out of all their troubles. The Lord is near to those who have a broken heart, And saves such as have a contrite spirit. Many are the afflictions of the righteous, But the Lord delivers him out of them all." – Psalm 34:17-19

The Final Step Is Death

""Oh, that You would hide me in Sheol (the nether world, the place of the dead), That You would conceal me until Your wrath is past, That You would set a definite time and then remember me [and in Your lovingkindness imprint me on your heart]! "If a man dies, will he live again? I will wait all the days of my struggle Until my change and release will come. "[Then] You will call, and I will answer You; You will long for [me] the work of Your hands. "But now You number [each of] my steps; You do not observe nor take note of my sin. "My transgression is sealed up in a bag, And You cover my wickedness [from Your view]. "But as a mountain, if it falls, crumbles into nothing, And as the rock is moved from its place, Water wears away the stones, Its floods and torrents wash away the soil of the earth, So You [O Lord] destroy the hope of man. "You prevail forever against him and overpower him, and he passes on; You change his appearance and send him away [from the presence of the living]. "His sons achieve honor, and he does not know it; They become insignificant, and he is not

aware of it. "But his body [lamenting its decay] grieves in pain over it, And his soul mourns over [the loss of] himself.""
- Job 14:13-22 AMP

Job is requesting that God allow death to claim him and that he be hidden there, away from the wrath of God until a set time. Job had poured everything out and now what he desired most was to die in peace, but even in his dying he knew that when God called him, he would rise up and give an account of his life. Intercessors I am sure that you have known someone who was ready and prepared to die. They made their peace with this world and with those that would be left behind once they were gone. When you die in God, then your eyes will search for his glorious resurrection where you will arise with a new body to life eternal.

"O Death, where is your sting? O Hades, where is your victory?" – 1 Corinthians 15:55 NKJV

God Answers Job's Prayers from A Whirlwind

Read Job 38:1-41. In this passage God begins speaking to Job and questioning him, not concerning his afflictions, but concerning his response to his afflictions. Like Job, none of us was around when God created the heavens and the earth. We were not there when He said, " Let there be light," and the light appeared. God created everything by the words of His mouth, and for this we should be grateful. After reading God's response to Job, and His rundown of His power and authority, it's just best to not say anything at all. God wins hands down.

I Have Nothing to Say

"Then the LORD said to Job, "Will the faultfinder contend with the Almighty? Let him who disputes with God answer it." Then Job replied to the LORD and said, "Behold, I am of little importance and contemptible; what can I reply to You? I lay my hand on my mouth. "I have spoken once, but I will not reply again-- Indeed, twice [I have answered], and I will add nothing further."" - Job 40:1-5 AMP

Intercessors there is nothing wrong with acknowledging where you are. You had only heard about the awesomeness of God, but now you have beheld it with your eyes, so take back whatever you said about Him that was not true and repent because now you have a better understanding of who God is.

I See and I Do Understand

"Then Job answered the LORD and said, "I know that You can do all things, And that no thought or purpose of Yours can be restrained. "[You said to me] 'Who is this that darkens and obscures counsel [by words] without knowledge?' Therefore [I now see] I have [rashly] uttered that which I did not understand, Things too wonderful for me, which I did not know. 'Hear, please, and I will speak; I will ask You, and You instruct [and answer] me.' "I had heard of You [only] by the hearing of the ear, But now my [spiritual] eye sees You. "Therefore I retract [my words and hate myself] And I repent in dust and ashes."" - Job 42:1-6 AMP

Now that Job has repented, God deals with his three friends who have wrongfully condemned Job. God sends them to Job to offer burnt offerings, so that Job could intercede on their behalf, because God would not accept their prayers since they had not spoken well on His behalf. The three friends do what the Lord requests and God accepts Job's prayer.

Intercessors, you must still pray for those that don't speak well of you and that have concluded within themselves that your afflictions are because of sin. Not So. Your intercession is needed so pray,pray,pray.

Chapter Seventeen

The Book of Psalms

The prayers that are listed in the Psalms can be prayed verbatim. Use them to strengthen you, encourage you, or to lift someone else's spirit. Here is an example of how to personalize the prayers in Psalms using Psalm 1:1-6.

"Blessed is the man who walks not in the counsel of the ungodly, Nor stands in the path of sinners, Nor sits in the seat of the scornful; But his delight is in the law of the Lord, And in His law he meditates day and night. He shall be like a tree planted by the rivers of water, That brings forth its fruit in its season, Whose leaf also shall not wither; And whatever he does shall prosper. The ungodly are not so, But are like the chaff which the wind drives away. Therefore the ungodly shall not stand in the judgment, Nor sinners in the congregation of the righteous. For the Lord knows the way of the righteous, But the way of the ungodly shall perish." - Psalm 1:1-6

Example:

Blessed is [Marnitha] because I don't walk in the counsel of the ungodly. I don't stand in the path of sinners. I don't sit in the seat of the scornful. [Marnitha's] delight is in the law of the Lord. And in his law [Marnitha] meditates day and night. [Marnitha] is like a tree that is planted by the rivers of water that brings forth its fruit in due season, whose leaf shall not wither and whatsoever [Marnitha] does will prosper. The ungodly are not so, but they are like the chaff which the wind drives away, therefore the ungodly shall not stand in judgment nor sinners in the congregation of the righteous for the Lord knows the way of the righteous, but the way of the ungodly shall perish.

Prayer for Total Trust In God- Psalm 4:1-8
Prayer of Protection- Psalm 5:1-12
Prayer for Mercy- Psalm 6:1-10
Prayer of Praise- Psalm 8:1-9
Prayer of Praise and Thanksgiving- Psalm 9:1-20
Prayer of the Lord As A Refuge- Psalm 11:1-7
Prayer of Worship- Psalm 19:1-14
Prayer for Victory- Psalm 20:1-9
Prayer of Praise for Help- Psalm 21:1-13
Prayer of Despair That Turns to Praise- Psalm 22:1-31
Prayer of Protection and Guidance- Psalm 25:1-20
Prayer for Thanksgiving- Psalm 30:1-12
Prayer of Forgiveness, Protection and Trust- Psalm 32:1-11
Prayer for Deliverance from Adversaries- Psalm 35:1-28
Prayer When Chastisement Is Given- Psalm 38:1-22
Prayer for Wisdom- Psalm 39:1-13
Prayer In Times of Sickness/Mistreatment- Psalm 41:1-13
Prayer for God's Presence- Psalm 42:1-11
Prayer of Rescue from Enemies- Psalm 43:1-5
Prayer of Remembrance- Psalm 44:1-26
Prayer to God As A Refuge of Safety- Psalm 46:1-11
Prayer of Repentance- Psalm 51:1-19
Prayer Concerning Treachery- Psalm 55:1-23
Prayer In Face of Adversity- Psalm 56:1-13
Prayer for Judgment of the Wicked- Psalm 58:1-11
Prayer of Lamentations Because of Defeat- Psalm 60:1-12
Prayer of Trust While Waiting on God- Psalm 62:1-12
Prayer of Deeper Fellowship with God- Psalm 63:1-11
Prayer of Blessing and Praise- Psalm 67:1-7
Prayer of the Goodness of God- Psalm 68:1-35

Conclusion

"Then [with a deep longing] you will seek Me and require Me [as a vital necessity] and [you will] find Me when you search for Me with all your heart." - Jeremiah 29:13 AMP

As you've read this book, it is my sincere hope that you have gathered some keys to empower you in your prayer life. I pray that from the flawed lives of the many men and women highlighted, you are both inspired and compelled to pray bold, audacious prayers. The Father is waiting to hear from you. May you continue to seek His face daily, and may He hear your prayers and answer.

Types of Prayer

Prayer of Supplication- Supplication means to petition or entreat someone or something. A passionate zeal and hunger fuels the prayer of supplication. Prayers of supplication should be prayed often as we earnestly desire to seek God's face and to know His will for our lives.

Prayer of Intercession- To intercede is to plead on behalf of another person. Intercessory prayer is prayer earnestly made for the needs of others, and seeking God's will for their life. We are called to intercede for others, just as Jesus intercedes for us.

Prayer of Faith- The prayer of faith is rooted in our confidence in God's word. When you are certain that what you are praying is the will of God, the prayer of faith can be employed. The prayer of faith is knowing God's will, praying it and receiving it from Him. Unforgiveness and doubt are the greatest hindrances to the prayer of faith.

Prayer of Agreement (Corporate Prayer)- The prayer of agreement is when two or more people come together and agree with one another and with the Word of God that something specific will be done.

Prayer of Praise & Thanksgiving- Praise and worship brings us into the presence of God. Praising God in both good times and bad affirms our faith in Him. Praise and thanksgiving are powerful weapons that disarm the two most deadly weapons in our Christian walk, unbelief and satanic attacks. These two things manifest differently, but praise and thanksgiving is the two-edged sword that helps us fight against evil.

Prayer of Blessings- To pray the prayer of blessings is to pray God's favor and protection.

Prayer of Worship- Similar to the prayer of thanksgiving, the prayer of worship focuses on who God is, while thanksgiving focuses on what He has done.

Prayer of Lament- Lament is a tool used by God's people to navigate pain and suffering. Lamenting enables us to petition God to deliver us from distress, suffering and pain. Prayers of lament are used to persuade God to act on the sufferer's behalf.

Prayer In the Spirit- To pray in the Spirit is to pray according to the Spirit's leading. It is praying for things that the Spirit leads us to pray for. Praying in the Spirit should be understood as praying in the power of the Spirit, by the leading of the Spirit, according to God's will.

Travailing Prayers- Travailing prayers are the manifestation of grief on the heart of God.

Prophetic Intercession- To prophetically intercede is to receive a sense of urgency from the Holy Spirit to pray for someone or something that is on the heart of God.

Made in the USA
Middletown, DE
10 September 2024